COLLINS

DIY

GUIDE

OUTDOORS & GARDENS

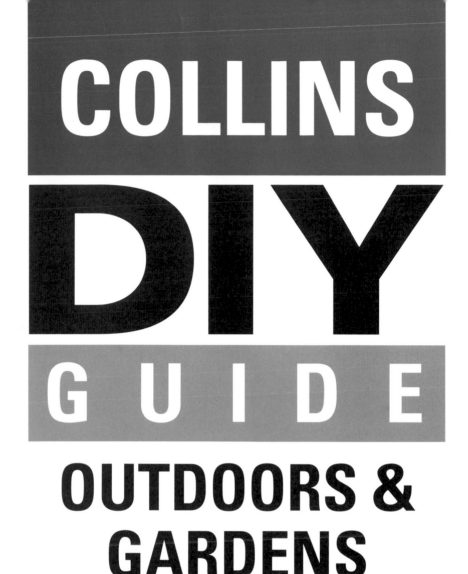

COLLINS
DIY
GUIDE

OUTDOORS & GARDENS

JACKSON·DAY

HarperCollinsPublishers

Published by
HarperCollins Publishers
London

This book was created exclusively
for HarperCollins Publishers by
Jackson Day Jennings Ltd
trading as Inklink.

Conceived, edited and designed
by Jackson Day Jennings Ltd
trading as Inklink.

Text
Albert Jackson
David Day

Editorial director
Albert Jackson

Text editors
Diana Volwes
Peter Leek

Executive art director
Simon Jennings

Design and art direction
Alan Marshall

Additional design
Amanda Allchin

Production assistant
Simon Pickford

Illustrations editor
David Day

Illustrators
Robin Harris
David Day

Additional illustrations
Brian Craker
Michael Parr
Brian Sayers

Photographers
Paul Chave
Karl Dietrich-Buhler
Jerry Harpur
Albert Jackson
Simon Jennings
Alan Marshall
Dr D. W. Davison
Neil Waving

Picture researchers
David Day
Anne-Marie Ehrlich
Hugh Olliff

Proofreaders
Mary Morton
Alison Turnball

For HarperCollins
Robin Wood – Managing Director
Polly Powell – Editorial Director
Bridget Scanlon – Production Manager

Consultants
The authors are grateful to the
following consultants for their
contributions and assistance.

Paul Cookson – Planning
John Dees and Bob Cole – Electricity

First published in 1988
This edition published in 1995

Most of the text and illustrations in
this book were previously published in
Collins Complete DIY Manual

ISBN 0 00 412767 6

Copyright © 1988, 1995
HarperCollins Publishers

The CIP catalogue record for this
book is available from the British
Library

Text set in Univers Condensed
and Bodoni
by Inklink, London

Imagesetting by
TD Studio, London

Colour origination by
Colourscan, Singapore

Printed and bound
in Hong Kong

Please note
Great care has been taken to
ensure that the information
contained in this **COLLINS DIY
GUIDE** is accurate. However, the
law concerning Building
Regulations, planning, local
bylaws and related matters is
neither static nor simple. A book
of this nature cannot replace
specialist advice in appropriate
cases and therefore no
responsibility can be accepted by
the publishers or by the authors
for any loss or damage caused by
reliance upon the accuracy of
such information.

Picture sources

Key to photographic credits
L = Left, R = Right, T = Top,
TL = Top left, TR = Top right,
C = Centre, UC = Upper centre,
LC = Lower centre, CL = Centre Left,
CR = Centre right, B = Bottom,
BL = Bottom left, BC = Bottom centre,
BR = Bottom right

Pat Brindley: 7CL, 53T
Cement & Concrete Association: 47
Paul Chave: 21, 22L, 24B, 32, 49, 51
Karl Dietrich-Buhler/EWA: 7B
Jerry Harpur/EWA: 7T
Albert Jackson:
6TR, 6BR, 20T, 24TR, 24CL, 24CR, 52UC,
52B, 55
Simon Jennings:
10, 11, 18, 19, 20UC, 20LC, 20B, 22R,
24TL, 25, 26, 37, 40, 50, 52T, 52LC, 69L
Alan Marshall 9
Original Box Sash Window Co Ltd: 63
Rentokil Ltd: 66, 68T, 68UC, 68LC, 69R
Harry Smith Collection:
6BL, 7CR, 53B, 57, 60
Waterways Ltd/Dr D. W. Davison: 62
Neil Waving: 70

CONTENTS

Cross-references

Since there are few DIY projects that do not require a combination of skills, you might have to refer to more than one section of this book. The list of cross-references in the margin will help you locate relevant sections or specific information related to the job in hand.

PLANNING
A GARDEN

SEE ALSO
Details for:
Building Regulations 72-73

Designing a garden is not an exact science. Plants may not thrive in a particular spot even though you select the right soil conditions and amount of daylight, and shrubs and trees may never reach the size specified for them in a catalogue. Nevertheless, forward planning will produce a more satisfactory result than a haphazard approach which could involve expensive mistakes like laying a patio where it will be in shade for most of the day or building a boundary wall that is too high to meet with official planning approval. It is these permanent features you should concentrate on planning first, always, of course, considering how they will fit into the planted and turfed areas of the garden.

Deciding on the approach

Before you even put pencil to paper, get a feel for the type of garden you would like and ask yourself whether it would sit happily with the house and its immediate surroundings. Is it to be a formal garden, laid out in straight lines or geometric patterns – a style which often marries successfully with modern architecture? Or do you prefer the more relaxed style of a rambling cottage garden? If you opt for the latter, bear in mind that natural informality may not be as easy to achieve as you think, and your planting scheme will certainly take several years to mature into the established garden you have in mind. You may prefer a blend of both styles, where every plant, stone and pool of water is carefully positioned; a Japanese-style garden bears all the hallmarks of a man-made landscape yet conveys a sense of natural harmony.

There is no shortage of material from which to draw inspiration, for there are countless books and magazines devoted to garden design. As no two gardens are alike you probably won't find a plan that fits your plot exactly, but you may be able to adapt a particular approach or develop a small detail into your own design. Visiting other gardens is an even better way of getting ideas. Large country estates and city parks will have been designed on a much grander scale, but at least you will be able to see how a mature shrub should look or how plants, stone and water have been used in a rockery or water garden. Don't forget that your friends may also have had to tackle problems identical to yours; if nothing else, you might learn by their mistakes!

A convincing rockery
(Top left)
Once plants become established, a rockery should blend into a garden without a hint of artificiality. The effect relies on the careful positioning of stones during its construction.

A simple layout
(Top right)
Simplicity is often the best approach, but the proportions of the various elements must be carefully considered to avoid a boring result.

Cottage-style garden
(Bottom left)
The informal character of abundant flowers planted around natural-stone or brick paths and over a rustic trellis ideally complements traditional cottage architecture.

Consider the details
(Bottom right)
Good design does not rely on having a large garden. A successful combination of natural forms can be just as rewarding on a small scale.

SURVEYING THE PLOT

Measuring the plot
Measure your plot of land as accurately as you can. Include the diagonal measurements, because a garden that appears to be exactly rectangular or square may not in fact be so.

Slopes and gradients
Make a note of how the ground slopes. An accurate survey is not necessary, but at least jot down the direction of the slope and plot the points where it begins and ends. You can get some idea of the differences in level by using a long straightedge and a spirit level. Place one end of the straightedge on the top of a bank, for example, and measure the vertical distance from the other end to the foot of the slope.

Climatic conditions
Check the passage of the sun and the direction of prevailing winds. Don't forget that the angle of the sun will be higher in summer and a screen of deciduous trees will be less of a windbreak when they drop their leaves.

Soil conditions
Make a note of soil conditions. You can easily adjust soil content by adding peat or fertilizers. A peat or clay soil is not very stable, however, and will affect the type of footings and foundations you may want to lay.

Existing features
Plot the position of features you want to retain in your plan, such as existing pathways, areas of lawn, established trees and so on.

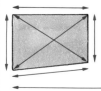

Measuring a plot
Note the overall dimensions including the diagonals to draw an accurate plan.

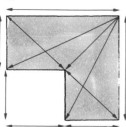

Gauging a slope
Use a straightedge and spirit level to measure the height of a bank.

SEE ALSO	
Details for:	
Footing/ foundations	29, 42
Retaining walls	39
Paving	48-53
Water gardens	57-61
Building a rockery	61

A formal garden
(Top)
Sculptured box hedges used to create regular patterns in traditional knot-garden style.

Using textures
(Centre left)
Still water punctuated with rugged stones makes for a pleasing contrast of textures.

A sloping site
(Centre right)
Some of the most dramatic gardens are a result of having to contend with a sloping site. Here retaining walls are used to terrace a steep bank of colourful shrubs.

Japanese-style garden
(Bottom)
Well-chosen plants with carefully placed natural stones and pebbles give an overall effect of tranquility.

BASIC CONSIDERATIONS

Having surveyed your plot, it is worth taking the time to plan all aspects of the design of your garden. Practical problems will need careful thought.

Drawing a plan

Draw a plan of your garden on paper. It must be a properly scaled plan or you are sure to make some gross errors, but it need not be professionally perfect. Use squared paper to plot the dimensions, but do the actual drawing on tracing paper laid over the graph paper so that you can try out several ideas and adapt your plan without having to redraw it every time.

Plotting your design

Planning on paper is only the first stage. Gardens are rarely seen from above so it is essential to plot the design on the ground to check your dimensions and view the features from different angles. A pond or patio which looks enormous on paper can be pathetically small in reality. Other shortcomings, such as the way a tree will block the view from your proposed patio, become obvious once you lay out the plan full-size.

Plot individual features by driving pegs into the ground and stretching string lines between them. Scribe arcs on the ground with a rope tied to a peg, and mark the curved lines with stakes or a row of bricks. Use a garden hose to mark out less regular curves and ponds. If you can scrape areas clear of weeds, it will define the shapes still further.

Practical experiments

When you have marked out your design, carry out a few experiments to check that it is practicable. Will it be possible, for instance, for two people to pass each other on the footpath without having to step into the flowerbeds? Can you set down a wheelbarrow on the footpath without one of its legs slipping into the pond?

Try placing some furniture on the area you have marked out for a patio to make sure you can relax comfortably and even sit down to a meal with visitors. Most people build a patio alongside the house, but if you have to put it elsewhere to find a sunny spot, will it become a chore to walk back and forth for drinks and snacks?

Siting ponds

Site a pond to avoid overhanging trees and in an area where it will catch at least half-a-day's sunlight. Check that you can reach it with a hose and that you can run electrical cables to power a pump or night-time lighting.

Common-sense safety

Don't make your garden an obstacle course. For example, a narrow path alongside a pond could be intimidating to an elderly relative, while low walls or planters near the edge of a patio could cause someone to trip.

Driveways and parking spaces

Allow a minimum width of 3m (9ft 9in) for a driveway, making sure there is enough room to open the car doors if you park alongside a wall. Remember that vehicles larger than your own might need to use the drive or parking space. Allow room for the turning circle of your car if possible and make sure that when you pull out into the road you will have a clear view of the traffic.

Consider the neighbours

There may be legal restrictions on what you can erect in your garden, but even if you have a free hand it is only wise to consult your neighbours if anything you plan might cause discomfort or inconvenience. A wall or even trees which are high enough to shade their favourite sunspot or block out the light to a window could be the source of argument for years to come.

Make a garden plan on tracing paper

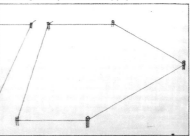
Mark out straight lines with pegs and string

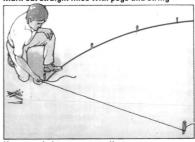
Use rope tied to a peg to scribe an arc

Try out irregular curves with a garden hose

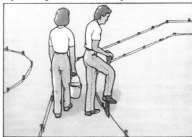
Make sure two people can pass on a path

TREE ROOTS AND FOUNDATIONS

SEE ALSO
Details for:
Pointing brickwork   32

As a permanent feature of your garden you will probably want to plant at least one tree. You will need to think carefully about your choice of trees and their position – they could be potentially damaging to the structure of the house if planted too near.

GROWING CLIMBERS

There is a widely held misconception that a climbing plant, especially ivy, will damage any masonry wall. If exterior rendering or the mortar between bricks or stonework is in a poor condition then an exuberant ivy plant will undoubtedly weaken the structure as its aerial roots attempt to extract moisture from the masonry. The roots invade broken joints or rendering and, on finding a source of nourishment for the main plant, expand and burst the weakened material, thus encouraging damp to penetrate. However, with sound bricks and mortar, ivy can do no more than climb by the aid of training wires and its own sucker-like roots which do not provide nourishment but are for support only. So long as the structure is sound and free from damp, there is some benefit from allowing a plant to clothe a wall in that its close-growing mat of leaves, mostly with their drip tips pointing downwards, acts as insulation and a watershed against the elements. Where ivy is permitted to flourish as a climber, it must be hard-pruned to prevent it penetrating between roof tiles or slates and clogging gutters and drainpipes. If any climber is allowed to grow unchecked, the weight of the mature plant may eventually topple a weakened wall.

Don't allow plants to get out of control

Cracks: subsidence and heave

Minor cracks in house plaster, rendering and even brickwork are often the result of shrinkage as the structure dries out. Such cracks are not serious and can be repaired during normal maintenance, but more serious structural cracks are due to movement of the foundations. Trees planted too close to a building can add to the problem by removing moisture from the site, causing subsidence of the foundations as the supporting earth collapses. Tree-felling can be just as damaging; the surrounding soil, which has become stabilized over the years, swells as it takes up the moisture which has been removed previously by the tree-root system. Upward movement of the ground, known as heave, distorts the foundations until cracks appear.

Siting trees

Tree roots search out moisture, which can result in an expensive repair or replacement of the house drainage system. Large roots can fracture rigid pipework or penetrate joints until the drain becomes blocked.

Before you plant a tree close to a building, find out the likely spread of the mature root system. As a rough guide, make sure there is a distance of at least two-thirds the mature height of a tree between it and nearby buildings. If an existing tree is likely to cause a problem, ask your local planning department for advice – the tree may be protected by a preservation order and you could be fined if you cut it down without permission. It may be possible to prune the branches and roots to lessen the likelihood of future damage.

Subsidence
A mature tree growing close to a house can draw so much water from the ground that the earth subsides, causing damage to the foundations.

Heave
When a mature tree is felled the earth can absorb more water, causing it to swell until it displaces the foundations of a building.

FENCES: CHOOSING

A fence is the most popular form of boundary marker or garden screen because of its advantages over other methods of dividing plots of land. A fence takes very little time to erect when compared with a wall and especially with a hedge, which takes years to establish. Most fencing components are relatively lightweight and are therefore easy to transport and handle on site.

Economics and maintenance

In the short term a fence is cheaper than a masonry wall, although one can argue that the cost of maintenance and replacement over a very long period eventually cancels out the saving in cost. Wood does have a comparatively short life because it is susceptible to insect infestation and rot when exposed to the elements, although a fence will last for many years if treated regularly with a preserver. If you are prepared to spend a little more money on plastic or concrete components, you can erect a virtually maintenance-free fence.

Chain-link fencing

Trellis fencing

Post-and-chain fence

Choosing your fencing

When you measure even a small garden you will be surprised by the overall length of fencing required to surround your property, so it is worth considering the available options carefully to make sure that you invest your money in the kind of fence that will be most suitable. Unless your priority is to keep neighbourhood children or animals out of your garden, the amount of privacy afforded by a fence is likely to be the most important consideration. There are a number of 'peep-proof' options, but you may have to compromise to some extent if you plan to erect a fence on a site exposed to strong prevailing winds. In that case you will need a fence which will provide a decent windbreak without offering such resistance that the posts will have worked loose within a couple of seasons of constant buffeting.

Planning and planning permission

You can build any fence up to 2m (6ft 6in) high without planning permission unless your boundary adjoins a highway, in which case you may not be able to erect a barrier higher than 1m (3ft 3in). In addition, there may be local restrictions on fencing if the land surrounding your house has been designed as an open-plan area. Even so, many authorities will permit low boundary markers such as a ranch-style or post-and-chain fence.

At least discuss your plans with your neighbours, especially as you will require their permission if you want to work from both sides when erecting a fence. Check the line of the boundaries to make certain that you do not encroach upon the neighbours' land. The fence posts should run along the boundary or on your side of the line, and before you dismantle an old fence make sure that it is indeed yours to demolish. If a neighbour is unwilling to replace an unsightly fence, or even to allow you to replace it at your expense, there is nothing to stop you erecting another fence alongside the original one provided it is on your property. It is an unwritten law that a good neighbour erects a fence with the post and rails facing his or her own property, but there are no legal restrictions which force you to do so.

TYPES OF FENCING

Chain-link fencing

Chain-link fencing is a utilitarian form of barrier constructed from wire netting stretched between fence posts. A true chain-link fence is made from strong galvanized or plastic-coated wire woven into a diamond-shape mesh, suspended from a heavy-gauge wire tensioned between the posts. You can make a cheap fence from soft wire netting or 'chicken wire', but it will not be durable and it will stretch if a large animal leans against it. Decorative wire fencing, which is available at many garden centres, is designed primarily for marking boundaries or supporting lightweight climbing plants. In fact, any chain-link fence will benefit from a screen of climbers or hedging plants.

Trellis fencing

A concertina-fold trellis formed from thin softwood or cedar laths joined together is virtually useless as a fence in the true sense, relying exclusively on the posts and rails for its strength. However, a similar fence made from split rustic poles nailed to stout rails and posts forms a strong and attractive barrier. Both types of trellis are ideally suited as plant supports for climbers.

Post-and-chain fencing

A post-and-chain fence is no more than a decorative feature which will prevent people inadvertently wandering off a path or pavement onto a lawn or flowerbed. They are constructed by stringing lengths of painted metal or plastic chain between short posts sunk into the ground.

TYPES OF FENCING

Closeboard fencing

A closeboard fence is made by nailing overlapping featherboard strips to horizontal rails. Featherboards are sawn planks which taper across their width from 16mm (⅝in) at the thicker side down to about 3mm (⅛in). The boards are 100mm (4in) or 150mm (6in) wide, and the best quality are made from cedar. However, softwood is the usual choice because of the high timber content of a closeboard fence. Although it is expensive, closeboard fencing forms a screen that is both strong and attractive. Because they are fixed vertically, the boards are quite difficult to climb from the outside – which makes them ideal for keeping children out!

Closeboard fencing

Prefabricated panel fencing

Fences made from prefabricated panels nailed between timber posts are very common, perhaps because they are particularly easy to erect. Standard panels are 1.8m (6ft) wide and range in height from approximately 600mm (2ft) to 1.8m (6ft); they are supplied in 300m (1ft) gradations. Most panels are made from interwoven or overlapping strips of larch sandwiched between a frame of sawn timber. The overlapping strip panels are usually designated 'larchlap', or, if the strips have a natural wavy edge, 'rustic larchlap'. You may also see them described as 'waney-edged', referring to where the thin strips of bark were, or may still be, attached to the planks.

A panel fence offers good value for money as a reasonably durable screen, but if privacy is a consideration choose the lapped type; interwoven strips will shrink to some extent in the summer, leaving gaps.

Panel fence

Interlap fencing

An interlap fence is made by nailing square-edged boards to the horizontal rails, fixing them alternately one side then the other. Spacing is a matter of choice. Overlap the edges of the boards for privacy, or space them apart for a decorative effect.

This is the type of fence to choose for a windy site as it is substantial yet the gaps between the boards allow the wind to pass through without exerting too much pressure. Because of its construction, an interlap fence is equally attractive from either side.

Interlap fencing

Picket fencing

The traditional low picket fence is still popular as a 'cottage-style' barrier at the front of the house where a high fence is unnecessary. Narrow, vertical 'pales' with rounded or pointed tops are spaced at 50mm (2in) centres. As they are laborious to build by hand, most picket fences are sold as ready-made panels constructed from plastic or softwood to keep down the cost.

Picket fencing

Ranch-style fencing

Low-level fences made from simple horizontal rails fixed to short, stout posts are the modern counterpart of picket fencing. Used extensively in some housing developments, this ranch-style fencing is often painted, although clear-finished or stained timber is just as attractive and far more durable. Softwoods and some hardwoods are used for this fencing; plastic ranch-style fences are also popular, both for their clean, crisp appearance and because they do not need to be repainted.

Ranch-style fence

Concrete fencing

A cast-concrete fence offers the security and permanence of a masonry wall and needs minimal maintenance. Interlocking horizontal sections are built one upon the other up to the required height. Each is supported by grooves cast into the sides of purpose-made concrete fence posts.

Concrete fencing

SEE ALSO
Details for:
Preservers   70

11

FENCE POSTS

Whatever type of fence you plan to erect, its strength and durability rely on good-quality posts set solidly in the ground. Buy the best posts you can afford, and erect them carefully. It is worth taking longer over its construction to avoid having to dismantle and repair a fence in the future.

TYPES OF POST

In some cases the nature of the fencing will determine the choice of post. Concrete fencing, for example, must be supported by compatible concrete posts, but, in the main, you can choose the material and style of post which suits the appearance of the fence.

Timber posts

Most fences are supported by square-section timber posts. Standard sizes are 75 and 100mm (3 and 4in) square, but 125, 150 and even 200mm (5, 6, 8in) square gate posts are available. Most timber merchants supply pretreated softwood posts unless you ask specifically for hardwood.

Concrete posts

A variety of 100mm (4in) square, reinforced-concrete posts exists to suit different styles of fence: drilled for chain-link fixings, mortised for rails and recessed or grooved for panels. Special corner and end posts are notched to accommodate bracing struts for chain-link fencing.

Metal posts

Angle-iron posts are made to support chain-link fences, and wrought-iron gates are often hung from plastic-coated tubular-steel posts. Angle-iron posts are very sturdy, but they do not make for an attractive fence.

Plastic posts

Extruded PVC posts are supplied with plastic fencing, together with moulded-plastic end caps and rail-fixing bolts and unions.

Preserving fence posts

Even when a timber fence post is pretreated to prevent rot, provide additional protection by soaking the base of each post in a bucket of chemical preserver for at least ten minutes and preferably longer.

Capping fence posts
If you simply cut the end of a timber post square, the top of the post will rot relatively quickly. The solution is to cut a single or double bevel to shed the rainwater, or nail a wooden or galvanized-metal cap over the end of the fence post.

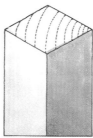

Square timber post

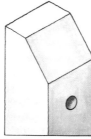

Drilled concrete post   **Mortised concrete post**

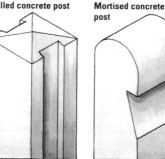

Grooved concrete post   **Notched end post**

Angle-iron post   **Tubular-steel post**

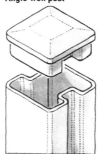

Capped plastic post

REMOVING OLD FENCE POSTS

Fixing posts in virgin soil is straightforward, but if you are replacing a fence you may want to put the new posts in the same position as the old. Remove the topsoil from around each post to loosen it. If one is bedded firmly, or sunk into concrete, lever it out with a stout batten. Drive large nails into two opposite faces of the post, about 300mm (1ft) from the ground. Bind a length of rope around the post just below the nails and tie the ends to the tip of the batten. Build a pile of bricks close to the post and use it as a fulcrum to lever the post out of the ground.

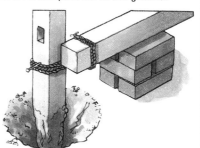

Levering a rotted fence post
Use a pile of bricks as a fulcrum to lift the post.

FIXING TO A WALL

If a fence runs up to the house, fix the first post to the wall with three expanding masonry bolts. Place a washer under each bolt head to stop the wood being crushed. Check that the post is vertical with a spirit level and drive packing between the post and wall to make any adjustments needed.

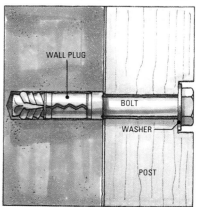

Bolting a post to a wall
If you are fitting a prefabricated panel against a wall-fixed post, counterbore the bolts so that the heads lie flush with the surface of the wood.

USING METAL SPIKES

Instead of anchoring fence posts in concrete, you can plug the base of each post into the square socket of a metal spike driven into firm ground. Use a 600mm (2ft) spike for fences up to 1.2m (4ft) high, and a 750mm (2ft 6in) spike for a 1.8m (6ft) fence.

Place a scrap of hardwood post into the socket to protect the metal, then drive the spike partly into the ground with a sledgehammer. Hold a spirit level against the socket to make certain the spike is upright (1), then hammer the spike into the ground until only the socket is visible. Insert the post and secure it by screwing through the side of the socket or by tightening clamping bolts (2), depending on the type of spike.

If you are erecting a panel fence, use the edge of a fixed panel to position the next spike (3).

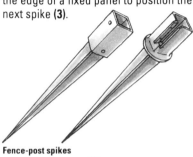
Fence-post spikes

1 Check a spike is vertical with a spirit level

2 Fix the post   **3 Position next spike**

The type of fence often dictates whether you erect all the posts first or one at a time along with the other components. When you are building a prefabricated panel fence, for example, fix the posts as you erect the fence – but complete the run of posts before you install chain-link fencing.

Marking out

Drive a peg into the ground at each end of the fence run and stretch a line between. If possible, adjust the spacing of the posts to avoid obstructions such as large tree roots. If one or more posts have to be inserted across a paved patio, lift enough slabs to dig the necessary holes. You may have to break up a section of concrete beneath the slabs using a cold chisel and hammer.

Erecting the posts

Digging the hole
Bury one quarter of each post to provide a firm foundation. For a 1.8m (6ft) high fence, dig a 600mm (2ft) hole to take a 2.4m (8ft) post. You can hire a post-hole auger to remove the central core of earth. Twist the tool to drive it into the ground (1) and pull it out after every 150mm (6in) to remove the soil. When you have reached a sufficient depth, taper the sides of the hole slightly so that you can pack hardcore and concrete around the post.

Anchoring the post
Ram a layer of hardcore (broken bricks or small stones) into the bottom of the hole to support the base of the post and provide drainage. Get someone to hold the post upright while you brace it with battens nailed to the post and to stakes driven into the ground (2). Use guy ropes to support a concrete post. Check with a spirit level that the post is vertical.

Ram more hardcore around the post, leaving a hole about 300mm (1ft) deep for filling with concrete. Mix some concrete to a firm consistency using the proportions 1 part cement : 2 parts sand : 3 parts aggregate. Use a trowel to drop concrete into the hole all round the post and tamp it down with the end of a batten (3). Build the concrete just above the level of the soil and smooth it to slope away from the post (4). This will help shed water and prevent rot. Leave the concrete to harden for about a week before removing the struts. To support a panel fence temporarily, wedge struts against the posts.

1 Dig the post hole   **2 Brace the post**   **3 Fill with concrete**   **4 Slope the concrete**

Supporting end posts

Chain-link fence posts must resist the tension of the straining wires. Brace each end post (and some intermediate ones over a long run) with a strut made from a length of fence post. Shape the end of the strut to fit a notch cut into the post (1) and nail it in place. Order special posts and precast struts for concrete components.

Anchor the post in the ground in the normal way, but dig a 450mm (1ft 6in) deep trench alongside for the strut. Wedge a brick under the end of the strut before ramming hardcore around the post and strut. Fill the trench up to ground level with concrete (2).

Support a corner post with two struts set at right angles. Where a fence adjoins a masonry wall, fix as described in the box opposite.

Post-hole auger

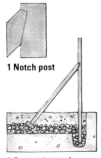
1 Notch post

2 Concreting end post

13

ERECTING A CHAIN-LINK FENCE

Set out a complete row of timber, concrete or angle-iron posts to support chain-link fencing, spacing them no more than 3m (10ft) apart. Brace the end posts with struts to resist the pull of the straining wires. A long run of fencing will need a braced intermediate post every 70m (225ft) or so.

Using timber posts

Support the chain-link fencing on straining wires (see right). As it is impossible to tension this heavy-gauge wire by hand, use large straining bolts to stretch it between the posts: one to coincide with the top of the fencing, one about 150mm (6in) from the ground, and the third midway between. Drill 10mm (⅜in) diameter holes right through the posts, insert a bolt into each hole and fit a washer and nut, leaving enough thread to provide about 50mm (2in) of movement once you begin to apply tension to the wire (**1**).

Pass the end of the wire through the eye of a bolt and twist it around itself with pliers (**2**). Stretch the wire along the run of fencing, stapling it to each post and strut, but leave enough slack for the wire to move when tensioned (**3**). Cut the wire to length and twist it through the bolt at the other end of the fence. Tension the wire from both ends by turning the nuts with a spanner (**4**).

Standard straining bolts provide enough tension for the average garden fence, but over a long run of fencing (70m (225ft) or more) use a turnbuckle for each wire, applying tension with a metal bar (see left).

Using concrete posts

Fix straining wires to concrete posts using a special bolt and cleat (see right). Bolt a stretcher bar to the cleats when erecting the wire netting.

Tie the straining wire to intermediate posts with a length of galvanized wire passed through the predrilled hole.

Using angle-iron posts

Winding brackets are supplied with angle-iron fence posts to attach stretcher bars and to apply tension to the straining wires (see right). As you pass the straining wire from end to end, pass it through the predrilled hole in every intermediate post.

Using a turnbuckle
Apply tension by turning the turnbuckle with a metal bar.

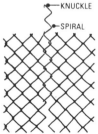
Joining wire mesh
Chain-link fencing is supplied in 25m (82ft) lengths. To join one roll to another, unfold the knuckles at each end of the first wire spiral, then turn the spiral anti-clockwise to withdraw it from the mesh. Connect the two rolls by rethreading the loose spiral in a clockwise direction through each link of the mesh. Bend the knuckle over at the top and bottom.

KNUCKLE
SPIRAL

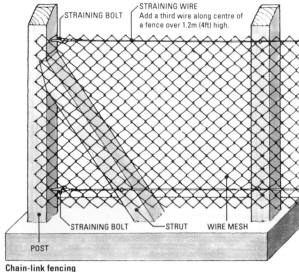
STRAINING BOLT
STRAINING WIRE
Add a third wire along centre of a fence over 1.2m (4ft) high.
STRAINING BOLT · STRUT · WIRE MESH
POST
Chain-link fencing

Attaching the mesh
Staple each end link to the post. Unroll the mesh and pull it taut. Tie it to straining wires every 300mm (1ft) with galvanized wire. Fix to the post at the far end.

Staple mesh to post

Tie with wire loops

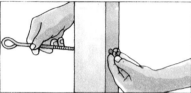
1 Insert a straining bolt in the end post

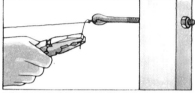
2 Attach a straining wire to the bolt

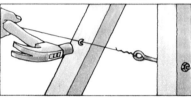
3 Staple the wire to the post and strut

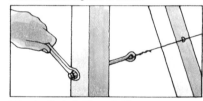
4 Tension the bolt at far end of fence

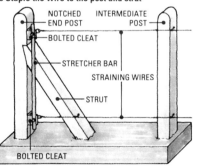
NOTCHED END POST
INTERMEDIATE POST
BOLTED CLEAT
STRETCHER BAR
STRAINING WIRES
STRUT
BOLTED CLEAT
Concrete fence posts

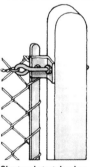
Cleat and stretcher bar

Tie wire to post

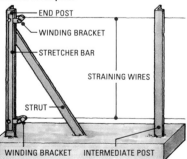
END POST
WINDING BRACKET
STRETCHER BAR
STRAINING WIRES
STRUT
WINDING BRACKET
INTERMEDIATE POST
Angle-iron posts

Winding bracket

Pass wire through post

ERECTING A CLOSEBOARD FENCE

The featherboards used to panel the fence are nailed to triangular-section rails known as arris rails. The arris rails are mortised into the fence posts. Concrete, and some wooden, posts are supplied ready-mortised, but if you buy standard timber posts you will have to cut the mortises. The end grain of the featherboards is liable to rot, especially if they are in contact with the ground, so fix horizontal 150 x 25mm (6 x 1in) gravel boards at the foot of the fence and nail wooden capping strips across the tops of the featherboards. Space the fence posts no more than 3m (10ft) apart.

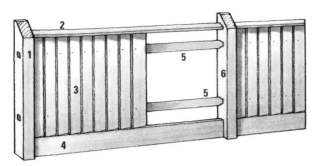

Closeboard fencing
1 End post
2 Capping strip
3 Featherboards
4 Gravel board
5 Arris rail
6 Intermediate post

REPAIRING A DAMAGED ARRIS RAIL

The arris rails take most of the strain when a closeboard fence is buffeted by high winds. Not surprisingly, they eventually crack across the middle or break where the tenon enters the mortise. Galvanized-metal brackets are available for repairing broken arris rails.

You can use end brackets to construct a new fence instead of cutting mortises for the rails. However, it will not be as strong as a fence built with mortise-and-tenon joints.

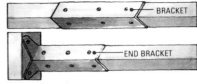

BRACKET

END BRACKET

Erecting the framework

If you are using plain wooden posts, mark and cut 50 x 22mm (2 x ⅞in) mortises for the arris rails about 150mm (6in) above and below the ends of the fixed featherboards. For fencing over 1.2m (4ft) high, cut mortises for a third rail midway between the others. Position the mortises 25mm (1in) from the front face of each post (the featherboarded side of the fence).

As you erect the fence, cut the rails to length and shape a tenon on each end with a coarse rasp or Surform file (1). Paint preserver onto the shaped ends and into the mortises before you assemble the rails.

Erect the first fence post and pack hardcore around its base. Get someone to hold the post steady while you fit the arris rails and erect the next post, tapping it onto the ends of the rails with a mallet (2). Check that the rails are horizontal and the posts are vertical before packing hardcore around the second post. Construct the entire run of posts and rails in the same way. If you cannot manoeuvre the last post onto tenoned rails, cut the rails square and fix them to the post with metal brackets (see box top right).

Check the whole run once more to ensure that the rails are bedded firmly in their mortises and the framework is true, then secure each rail by driving a nail through the post into the tenon (3) or drilling a hole and inserting a wooden dowel. Pack concrete around each post. Leave to harden for about a week.

Fitting the boards

Gravel boards

Some concrete posts are mortised to take gravel boards; fit them at the same time as the arris rails. If the posts are not mortised, bed wooden cleats into the concrete filling at the base of the post and screw the board to the cleat when the concrete is set.

To fit gravel boards to wooden posts, skew-nail treated wooden cleats at the foot of each post, then nail the boards to the cleats (4).

Featherboards

Cut the featherboards to length and treat the end grain. Stand the first board on the gravel board with its thick edge against the post. Nail the board to the arris rails with galvanized nails set 18mm (¾in) from the thick edge. Place the next board in position, overlapping the thin edge of the fixed board by 12mm (½in). Check that it is vertical, then nail it in the same way. Don't drive a nail through both boards or they won't be able to move when they shrink. To space the other boards equally, make a spacer block from a scrap of wood (5). Place the last board to fit against the next post and fix it, this time with two nails per rail (6). When the fence is completed, nail capping strips across the tops of the featherboards, cut the posts to length and cap them.

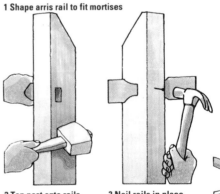

1 Shape arris rail to fit mortises

2 Tap post onto rails

3 Nail rails in place

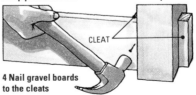

CLEAT

4 Nail gravel boards to the cleats

5 Use a spacer block to position featherboards

6 Fix last board with two nails

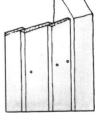

Capping the fence
Nail a wooden capping strip to the ends of the featherboards to shed rainwater.

ERECTING A PANEL FENCE

To prevent a prefabricated panel rotting, either fit gravel boards as for a closeboard fence, or leave a gap at the bottom by supporting a panel temporarily on two bricks while you nail it to the fence posts.

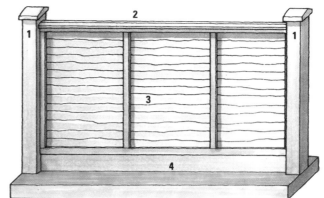

Panel fence
1 Fence posts
2 Capping strip
3 Prefabricated panel
4 Gravel board

Using timber posts

Pack the first post into its hole with hardcore, then get someone to hold a panel against the post while you skew-nail through its framework into the post (**1**). If you can work from both sides, drive three nails from each side of the fence. If the frame starts to split, blunt the nails by tapping their points with a hammer. Alternatively, use metal angle brackets to secure the panels (**2**). Construct the entire fence erecting panels and posts alternately.

Nail capping strips across the panels if they have not already been fitted by the manufacturer. Finally, cut each post to length and cap it.

Wedge struts made from scrap timber against each post to keep it vertical, then top up the holes with concrete. If you are unable to work from both sides, you will have to fill each hole as you build the fence.

Using concrete posts

Grooved concrete posts will support panels without the need for additional fixings (**3**). Recessed concrete posts are supplied with metal brackets for screw-fixing the panels (**4**).

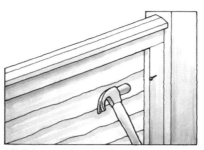

1 Nail the panel through its framework

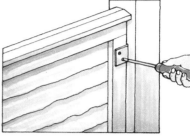

2 Or use angle brackets to fix panel to posts

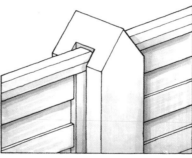

3 A grooved concrete post for a fence panel

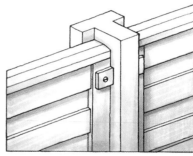

4 A recessed concrete post with fixing bracket

Building a panel fence
Posts and panels are erected alternately. Dig a hole for the post (**1**) and hold it upright with hardcore. Support a panel on bricks (**2**) and have a helper push it against the post (**3**)

while you nail it (**4**). Fit gravel boards (**5**), capping strips (**6**) and cap the posts (**7**). Top up the holes with concrete (**8**) and allow it to set.

ERECTING A POST-AND-RAIL FENCE

A simple ranch-style fence is no more than a series of horizontal rails fixed to short posts concreted into the ground in the normal way. A picket fence is made in a similar way, but with vertical pales fixed to the rails.

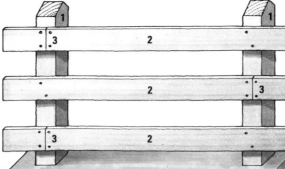
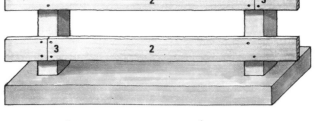

Ranch-style fence
1 Short posts
2 Horizontal rails
3 Rail joints

Fixing horizontal rails

You can simply screw the rails directly to the posts (1), but the fence will last longer if you cut a shallow notch in the post to locate each rail before you fix it permanently (2).

Join two rails by butting them over a post (3). Arrange to stagger these joints so that you don't end up with all the rails butted on the same post (4).

Fixing picket panels

When you construct a picket fence from ready-made panels, buy or make metal brackets for fixing two panels to a single post.

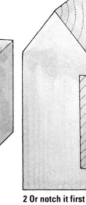

1 Screw rail to post

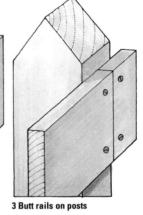

2 Or notch it first

3 Butt rails on posts

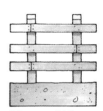

4 Stagger rail joints

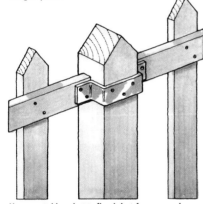

Use a metal bracket to fix picket-fence panels

Supporting a rotted post

A buried timber post will quite often rot below ground level, leaving a perfectly sound section above. To save buying a whole new post, brace the upper section with a concrete spur.

Erecting a spur
Dig the soil from around the post and remove the rotted stump. Insert the spur and pack hardcore around it (1), then fill with concrete (2). Drill pilot holes for coach screws – woodscrews with hexagonal heads (3). Insert the screws with a spanner to draw the post tightly against the spur.

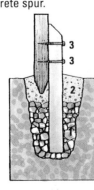

ERECTING FENCES ON SLOPING GROUND

Crossways slope
If a slope runs across the garden, so that your neighbour's garden is higher than yours, build brick retaining walls between the posts or set paving stones in concrete to hold back the soil.

Downhill slope
The posts must be set vertically even when you erect a fence on a sloping site. Chain-link fencing or ranch-style rails can follow the slope of the land if you wish, but fence panels should be stepped and the triangular gaps beneath filled with gravel boards or retaining walls.

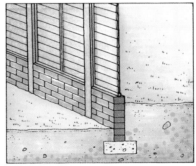

A retaining wall for a crossways slope

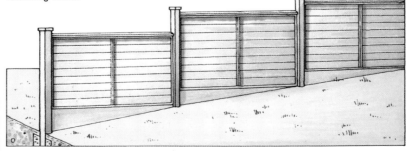

Step fence panels to allow for a downhill slope

● **Building plastic fences**
The basic construction of a plastic ranch-style fence is similar to one built from timber, but follow the manufacturer's instructions concerning the method for joining rails to posts.

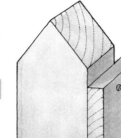

17

GATES:
CHOOSING

There are several points to consider when choosing a gate, not the least the cost. All gates are relatively expensive, but don't buy one merely because it is cheaper than another; a gate must be sturdy if it is to be durable. It must also be mounted on strong posts.

    Choose a style of gate which matches the fence or complements the wall from which it is hung, with due consideration for the character of the house and its surroundings. If in doubt, aim for simplicity.

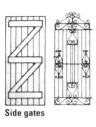

Side gates

Entrance gates

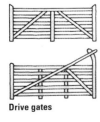

Drive gates

GATES FOR DIFFERENT LOCATIONS

When you browse through suppliers' catalogues you will find gates grouped according to their intended location, because it is where it is to be sited that has most influence on the design of a gate and which dictates its function.

Side gates

A side gate is designed to protect a pathway next to a house from intruders. Side gates are invariably 2m (6ft 6in) high and are made from wrought iron or stout sections of timber. Wooden gates are heavy and are therefore braced with strong diagonal members to keep them rigid. With security in mind, choose a closeboarded or tongued-and-grooved gate as vertical boards are difficult to climb. When you hang a side gate, fit strong bolts top and bottom.

Entrance gates

An entrance gate is designed as much for its appearance as its function, but because it is in constant use, make sure it is properly braced with a diagonal strut running from the top of the latch stile down to the bottom of the hanging or hinge stile. If you hang a gate with the strut running the other way, the bracing will have no effect whatsoever.

    Common fence structures are reflected in the style of entrance gates. Picket, closeboard and ranch-style gates are available, plus a simple and attractive frame-and-panel gate. With the latter style of gate, the solid timber or exterior-grade plywood panels keep the frame rigid. If the tops of both stiles are cut at an angle they will shed rainwater, reducing the likelihood of wet rot – a small, but important, feature to note when buying a wooden gate.

    Decorative iron gates are often used for entrances, but make sure the style is not too ostentatious for the building or its location. A very elaborate gate might look ridiculous in the entrance of a simple modern house or a traditional country cottage.

Drive gates

First decide whether hanging a gate across a drive to a garage is a good idea. Parking the car in a busy road in order to open the gate can be a difficult manoeuvre unless you have enough room to set the gate back from the entrance, leaving enough space to pull the car off the road even when the gate is closed. Gates invariably open into the property, so make sure there is enough ground clearance for a wide gate if the drive slopes up. An alternative is to hang two smaller gates to meet in the centre. If you decide on a wide gate, choose a traditional five-bar gate for both strength and appearance.

Gate posts and piers

Gate posts and masonry piers have to take a great deal of strain, so they must be both strong and anchored securely in the ground.

    Choose hardwood posts whenever possible, and select the section according to the weight of the gate: 100mm (4in) square posts are adequate for entrance gates, but use 125mm (5in) posts for 2m (6ft 6in) high gates. For a gate across a drive, choose 150mm (6in) or even 200mm (8in) square posts.

    Concrete posts are a possibility, but unless you find a post predrilled to accept hinges and catch, you will have to screw them to a strip of timber bolted securely to the post.

    Square or cylindrical tubular-steel metal posts are available with hinge pins, gate-stop and catch welded in place. Like metal gates, they must be protected from rust with paint unless they have been coated with plastic at the factory.

    A pair of masonry piers is another possibility. Each pier should be a minimum of 328mm (1ft 1½in) square and built on a firm concrete footing. For large, heavy gates, the hinge pier at least should be reinforced with a metal rod buried in the footing and running centrally through the pier.

HARDWARE FOR GATES

A range of specialized hardware has been developed to allow for the considerable strain that a garden gate imposes on its hinges and catch.

Hinges

Strap hinges
Side gates and most wooden entrance gates are hung on strap hinges, or T-hinges. Screw the long flap horizontally to the gate rails and the vertical flap to the face of the post. Heavier gates need a stronger version bolted through the top rail.

Wide drive gates need a double strap hinge with a long flap bolted on each side of the top rail. These heavy-duty hinges are supported by bolts which pass through the gate post.

Hinge pins
Metal collars, welded to the hinge side of metal gates, drop over hinge pins attached to gate posts in a variety of ways: screw-fixed to timber posts; bolted through concrete; built into the mortar joints of masonry piers; welded to metal posts. The gate can be lifted off its hinges at any time unless you reverse the top pin or drill a hole and fit a split pin and washer.

Latches

Automatic latches
Simple wooden gates are fitted with a latch that operates automatically as the gate is closed. Screw the latch bar to the latch stile of the gate and use it to position the latch on the post.

Thumb latches
Cut a slot through a closeboard side gate for the latch lifter of a thumb latch. Pass the lifter bar (sneck) through the slot and screw the handle to the front of the gate. Screw the latch beam to the inner face so that the sneck releases the beam from the hooked keeper.

Ring latches
A ring latch works in a similar way to a thumb latch, but is operated from inside only by twisting the ring handle to lift the latch beam.

Chelsea catches
Bolt a Chelsea catch through a drive gate. The latch pivots on the bolt to drop into a slot in the catch plate screwed to the post.

Loop-over catches
When two wide gates are used in a drive entrance, one gate is fixed with a drop bolt located in a socket concreted into the ground. A simple U-shaped metal bar, bolted through the latch stile of the other gate, drops over the stile of the fixed gate.

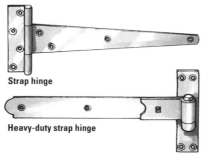
Strap hinge

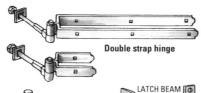
Heavy-duty strap hinge

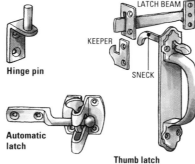
Double strap hinge

LATCH BEAM

KEEPER

SNECK

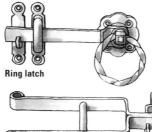
Hinge pin

Automatic latch

Thumb latch

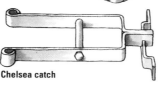
Ring latch

Chelsea catch

Loop-over catch

Materials for gates

Many wooden gates are made from relatively cheap softwood, but a wood such as cedar or oak is a better investment. Most so-called wrought-iron gates are made from mild-steel bar which must be primed and painted if it is to last any time at all.

Hang a heavy drive gate on a stout post

Gate posts are set in concrete like ordinary fence posts, but the post holes are linked by a concrete bridge to provide extra support.

Entrance-gate posts

Lay the gate on the ground with a post on each side. Check that the posts are parallel and the required distance apart to accommodate hinges and catch. Nail two horizontal battens from post to post and another diagonally to keep the posts in line while you erect them (1).

Dig a 300mm (1ft) wide trench across the entrance. Make it long enough to accept both posts. It need be no deeper than 300mm (1ft) in the centre, but dig an adequate post hole at each end: 450mm (1ft 6in) deep for a low entrance gate; 600mm (2ft) deep for a taller side gate. Set the battened gate posts in the holes with hardcore and concrete as for fence posts, using temporary battens to hold them upright until the concrete sets (2). Fill the trench with concrete at the same time and either level it flush with the pathway or allow for the thickness of paving slabs or blocks.

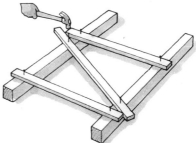
1 Nail temporary struts to the gate posts

2 Support the posts until the concrete sets

Drive-gate posts

Hang wide farm-style gates on posts set in 900mm (3ft) deep holes (3). Erect the latch post in concrete like any fence post, but bolt a stout piece of timber across the base of the hinge post before anchoring it in concrete.

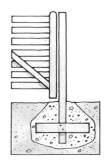
3 Drive-gate post
Bolt a balk of timber to the post to help support the weight of the gate.

MASONRY:
BUILDING
WALLS

Whatever structure you build with masonry, the basic techniques for laying brick, stone or concrete blocks remain the same. It pays to hire a professional builder when the structure is complicated or extensive, or if it will have to bear considerable loads or stress.

A stone-built retaining wall

A boundary wall of yellow brick

Facing blocks make attractive dividing walls

A decorative pierced-block screen

Amateur bricklaying

It is difficult to suggest when a particular job is beyond the level of skill or confidence of an amateur bricklayer as this differs from one individual to another. It would be foolhardy for anyone to attempt to build a two-storey house, for example, unless they had had a lot of experience and, possibly, professional tuition; even building a high boundary wall, which in terms of pure technique is simple, would be an arduous task if it were very long or had to allow for changes in gradient. The simple answer is to begin with low retaining or dividing walls and screens until you have mastered the skills of laying bricks and blocks solidly upon one another, and developed the ability to build a wall that is sound, straight and absolutely vertical.

WALLS FOR DIFFERENT LOCATIONS

Retaining walls

Raised planting beds are made by means of low 'retaining' walls, although a true retaining wall is designed to hold back a bank of earth, usually to terrace a sloping site. Provided it is not too high a retaining wall is quite easy to build, although strictly speaking it should slope back into the bank to resist the weight of the earth. You must also allow for drainage in order to reduce the water pressure behind the wall. Retaining walls are built with bricks, concrete blocks or stone, and are sometimes dry-laid with earth packed into the crevices for planting – it is a matter of personal choice.

Boundary walls

A brick or stone wall surrounding your property provides security and privacy while forming an attractive background to trees and shrubs. New brickwork complements a formal garden or modern setting, while second-hand materials or undressed stone blend well with an old, established garden. If you cannot quite match the colour of existing masonry, encourage the growth of lichen with a wash of liquid fertilizer or disguise the junction with a climbing plant. You will need to apply for local-authority approval if you want to build a wall higher than 1m (3ft 3in) adjoining a highway or 2m (6ft 6in) elsewhere.

Dividing walls

Many gardeners divide a plot of land with walls to form a visual break between patio and lawn, to define the edges of pathways, or simply to add interest to an otherwise featureless site. Dividing walls are often merely 'dwarf' walls, perhaps 600 to 750mm (2 to 2ft 6in) in height.

Use simple concrete block or brick walls to divide spaces inside your workshop or garage.

Screen walls

Screens are also dividing walls, which provide a degree of privacy without completely masking the garden beyond. They are built with decorative pierced blocks, often with solid-block or brick bases and concrete piers.

Structural walls

The walls of even a small building have to support the weight of a roof and, depending on the complexity of the structure, incorporate doorframes and window frames. In most cases a damp-proof course will have to be built into the walls to prevent rising damp; some walls are constructed with a cavity between two leaves of masonry to provide insulation and weatherproofing. A brick foundation for a glazed conservatory is no more difficult to build than a simple garden wall, but make certain you are familiar with building methods before you attempt to build a garage or similar outbuilding.

The names given to bricks refer to their district of origin, where a particular clay will impart a distinctive colour, or are simply chosen by the manufacturer to suggest the continuation of that tradition. Typical examples are London stocks, Pennines, Leicester reds, Blue Staffs and so on. What is important to the builder is the variety, quality and type of brick, and, particularly when matching existing masonry, the colour and texture.

The variety of brick

Facings
Facings are suitable for any type of exposed brickwork. They are water-resistant and frost-resistant. Being visible, facings are made as much for their appearance as their structural qualities and, as such, are available in a wide range of colours and textures. They are made to specific standards of strength and water-absorption and are uniform in size.

Commons
Commons are cheap general-purpose bricks used primarily for internal brickwork which is to be plastered, or rendered if used externally. They are not colour-matched as carefully as facings, but the mottled effect of a wall built with commons is not unattractive.

Although they could be damaged by frost if used on an exposed site, commons are sometimes employed for garden walling.

Engineering bricks
Engineering bricks are exceptionally dense and strong. You are unlikely to need them for the average wall, but, because they are impervious to water, they have been used to construct a damp-proof course in some houses.

The quality of brick

Internal quality
Internal-quality bricks would not be very durable if they were exposed to weathering. Most commons are of internal quality only, so check before you buy them for use in the garden.

Ordinary quality
Ordinary-quality bricks are suitable for most external uses. They may suffer, however, if used for a wall exposed to frequent driving rain and frost, or for a retaining wall which holds back earth that is poorly drained.

Special quality
Special-quality bricks will withstand extreme weathering and frost. Most types of facing brick are available in this quality; they are especially suitable for walls in coastal areas.

Seconds
Seconds are second-hand rather than second-rate bricks. They should be cheaper than new bricks, but demand can inflate the price. Using seconds might be the only way you can match the colour of weathered brickwork.

Types of brick

Solid bricks
The majority of bricks are solid throughout, either flat on all surfaces or with a depression known as a 'frog' on one face. When filled with mortar, the frog keys the bricks.

Cored or perforated bricks
Cored bricks have holes through them, providing the same function as the frog. A wall made with cored bricks must be finished with a coping of solid bricks.

Special shapes
Specially shaped bricks are made for decorative brickwork. Master bricklayers use the full range to build arches, chamfered or rounded corners and curvilinear walls. A number of shaped bricks are made for coping garden walls.

BUYING BRICKS

Ordering bricks
Bricks are normally sold by the thousand, but builders' merchants are usually willing to sell them in smaller quantities. It is cheaper to order them direct from the manufacturer, but only if you buy a sufficient load to make the delivery charge economical.

Estimating quantities
The size of a standard brick is 215 x 102.5 x 65mm (8½ x 4 x 2½in), but dimensions may vary by a few millimetres, even within the same batch of bricks. Manufacturers normally specify a nominal size which includes an additional 10mm (⅜in) to each dimension to allow for the mortar joint.

To calculate how many bricks you need, allow about 58 bricks for every square metre (48 per sq yd) of single-skin walling. Add a five per cent allowance for cutting and breakages.

Storing bricks
When the bricks are delivered, stack them carefully on a flat, dry base. Cover the bricks with polyethylene sheet or a tarpaulin until you are ready to use them in order to prevent them becoming saturated with rain, which could cause staining as well as an increased risk of frost damage to the mortar and the bricks themselves.

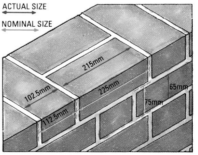

ACTUAL SIZE

NOMINAL SIZE

215mm
225mm
102.5mm
112.5mm
65mm
75mm

Nominal and actual size of bricks

Types of brick

DOUBLE-CANT COPING
STANDARD BRICK WITH FROG
SQUINT FOR SHAPED CORNER
STANDARD CORED BRICK
BULLNOSE
HALF-ROUND COPING

THE COLOUR AND TEXTURE OF BRICKS

The popularity of brick as a building material stems largely from its range of subtle colours and textures, which actually improve with weathering. Weathered brick can be difficult to match by using a manufacturer's catalogue, so try to borrow samples from your supplier's stock or, if you have spare bricks, take one to the supplier to compare it with new bricks.

Colour

The colour of bricks is determined by the type of clay used in their manufacture, although it is modified by the addition of certain minerals and the temperature of the firing. Large manufacturers supply a wide variety of colours and there are also brindled (multi-coloured or mottled) bricks that are especially useful for blending with existing masonry.

Texture

Texture is as important to the appearance of a brick wall as colour. Simple rough or smooth textures are created by the choice of materials. Others are imposed upon the clay by scratching, rolling, brushing and so on. A brick may be textured all over or on the sides and ends only.

Brick colours and textures
A small selection from the extremely wide range of colours and textures.
1 Smooth blended
2 Handmade
3 Sand-faced yellow
4 Smooth blue engineering
5 Sand-faced grey
6 Smooth red stock
7 Wire-cut brindle
8 Textured multi-buff
9 Second London stock
10 Wire-cut blue
11 Red common
12 Coarse fletton
13 Moulded fletton
14 Dragwire multi-red

Pattern formed by projecting headers

Decorative combination of coloured bricks

Look out for second-hand moulded bricks

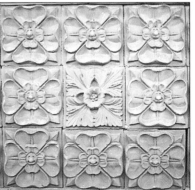

Sometimes whole panels are available

Weathered antique bricks are very attractive

Cast-concrete building blocks are not as standardized as clay bricks, but describing them under the same specifications – that is, variety, quality and type – makes for a handy comparison when choosing which to use.

The variety of block

Structural blocks
Simple rectangular blocks, cement-grey or white in colour, are used as the structural core of a wall which will be rendered or plastered. Consequently, they are often made with a zig-zag key on the surface. As they are not intended to be visible, they have no aesthetic qualities at all. A wall can be built quickly with blocks because they are much larger than standard housebricks, and the cost will be relatively low.

Facing blocks
These are blocks with one decorative face and end for walls which are to be left exposed. They are often made to resemble natural stone by including crushed-stone aggregate. There is a range of colours to blend with the local stone in most areas of the country. Facing blocks are used for the external skin of cavity walls, backed by the cheaper structural blocks. They are also used for ornamental garden walling, for which matching coping slabs are available as a finishing touch.

Screen blocks
Screen blocks are pierced decorative building units for constructing a lightweight masonry trellis or screen. They are not bonded like brickwork or structural blocks and therefore require supporting piers made from matching pilaster blocks with locating channels to take the pierced blocks. Coping slabs finish the top of the screen and piers.

The quality of block

Loadbearing blocks
Structural blocks are used to construct the loadbearing walls of a building. Those made with lightweight aggregate are easier to handle, but when the loads are excessive, use stronger blocks made from dense concrete.

Non-loadbearing blocks
Non-loadbearing blocks are used to build internal, dividing partitions. They are either lightweight-aggregate blocks or low-density foamed-concrete blocks which are easy to cut to shape or chase for electrical wiring. Foamed blocks are also made in a loadbearing quality.

Decorative blocks
Screen blocks should not be used in the construction of loadbearing walls. However, they are capable of supporting a lightweight structure such as a timber-and-plastic carport roof.

Insulating blocks
Foamed blocks are often used for constructing the inner leaf of a cavity wall. They have good insulating properties and meet the minimum Building Regulation standards without the need for secondary insulation. Use ultra-light foamed blocks when improved insulation is required.

Types of block

Solid blocks
Solid blocks are constructed either with lightweight aggregate or with foamed concrete.

Cored blocks
To reduce their weight, large dense-concrete blocks are virtually hollow with supporting ribs between the outer skins. Stretcher blocks are used for the main part of the wall, while corner blocks are used when the end of a wall is exposed. The hollows can be reinforced with concrete. Solid-top blocks, partly hollowed out on the underside, are used to support joists.

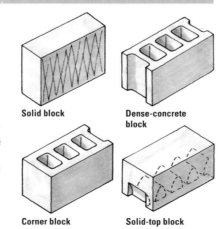

Solid block

Dense-concrete block

Corner block

Solid-top block

BUYING CONCRETE BLOCKS

Estimating quantities
Blocks are available in such a variety of sizes that in order to calculate the number required you must divide a given area of walling by the dimensions of a specific type. Blocks are sometimes specified in nominal sizes (also known as coordinating sizes), but with 10mm (⅜in) allowance for mortar on the length and height only. Block walls are normally constructed with one skin of masonry, so the thickness of a block remains as the actual size.

Available sizes
Structural blocks are normally 450mm (1ft 6in) long, with heights of 150 to 225mm (6 to 9in). Actual thicknesses range from 75 to 300mm (3 to 12in).

Although larger sizes are available, facing blocks are normally 100mm (4in) thick, with lengths of between 225 and 450mm (9in and 1ft 6in) and heights of between 75 and 150mm (3 and 6in).

Decorative screen blocks are invariably 300mm (1ft) square and 90mm (3½in) thick.

Storing blocks
When blocks are delivered have them unloaded as near as possible to the construction site to save time and reduce the possibility of damage in transit – they are quite brittle and chip easily. Stack them on a flat, dry base and protect them from rain and frost with a polyethylene sheet or tarpaulin.

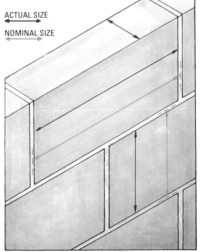

ACTUAL SIZE

NOMINAL SIZE

Sizes of structural blocks
The nominal size of a block refers to the length and height only. Thicknesses are always specified as an actual size.

BLOCKS AND STONES

Man-made blocks made from poured concrete are available in a variety of colours, shapes and sizes. Aesthetically, however, nothing can surpass quarried stone such as granite or sandstone. Whether it be roughly hewn or finely dressed, natural stone is durable and weathers well.

Semi-dressed natural-stone blocks

Dry-stone retaining wall

Man-made concrete blocks
1 Solid dense concrete
2 Lightweight aerated
3 Lightweight aggregate
4 Pierced decorative
5 Solid decorative
6 Pitched-face reconstituted stone
7 Pilaster block
8 Pilaster coping
9 Multi-stone block
10 Screen coping
11 Split-face facing
12 Hewn-stone facing

Split-stone walling

Knapped-flint boundary wall

CHOOSING NATURAL STONE

Practical considerations
In practical terms, the type of natural stone you choose for walling depends almost entirely on where you happen to live. In some parts of the country there are local restrictions governing the choice of building materials, and, in any case, a structure built from stone that is indigenous to the locality is more likely to blend into its surroundings. Buying stone from a local quarry also makes economical sense – transporting stone over long distances can be very costly.

Where to obtain stone
If you live in a large town or city, obtaining natural stone can be a real problem. You might be prepared to buy a few small boulders for a rockery from a local garden centre, but the cost of buying enough stone for even a short run of walling is likely to be prohibitive. If you don't want to use reconstituted stone – concrete facing blocks – your only alternative is to hire an open truck and drive to a quarry out of town.

Another source of materials, and possibly the cheapest way to obtain dressed stone, is to visit a demolition site. Prices vary considerably, but the cost of transport may be less than a trip to a quarry.

Estimating quantities
Most quarries sell stone by the tonne. When you have worked out the dimensions of the wall, telephone the nearest quarry for advice on quantity and a quote for the cost of the stone. Once you know the quantity you need you will be able to hire a truck of the appropriate capacity.

Types of stone
Limestone, sandstone and granite are all suitable materials for building walls. Flint and slate require specialized building methods and are often used in combination with other materials. Stone bought in its natural state is classed as random rubble (undressed); it is perfect for dry-stone walling in an informal garden setting. For a more regular form of masonry, ask for squared rubble (semi-dressed) stone which is cut into reasonably uniform blocks but with uneven surfaces, or ashlar (fully dressed stone with machine-cut faces). The cost of stone increases in proportion to its preparation.

MASONRY
CLEANING

CLEANING
BRICK AND
STONE
SEE ALSO

Before you decorate the outside of your house, check the condition of the brick and stonework and carry out any necessary repairs. Unless you live in an area of the country where there is a tradition of painting brick and stonework, you will probably want to restore painted masonry to its original condition. Although most paint strippers cannot cope with deeply textured surfaces, there are thick-paste paint removers that will peel away layers of old paint from masonry walls.

Stained brickwork

Organic growth

Efflorescence

Treating new masonry

New brickwork or stonework should be left for about three months until it is completely dry before any further treatment is considered. White powdery deposits called efflorescence may come to the surface over this period, but you can simply brush them off with a stiff-bristle brush or a piece of dry sacking. Masonry is weatherproof and therefore requires no further treatment, except that in some areas of the country you may wish to apply paint.

Cleaning organic growth from masonry

There are innumerable species of mould growth and lichens which first appear as tiny coloured specks or patches on masonry. They gradually merge until the surface is covered with colours that range from bright orange to yellow, green, grey and black.

Moulds and lichen will only flourish in damp conditions, so try to cure the source of the problem before treating the growth. If one side of the house always faces away from the sun, for example, it will have little chance to dry out. Relieve the situation by cutting back any overhanging trees or shrubs to increase ventilation to the wall.

Make sure the damp-proof course (DPC) is working adequately and is not being bridged by piled earth or debris.

Cracked or corroded rainwater pipes leaking on to the wall are another common cause of organic growth. Feel behind the pipe with your fingers or slip a hand mirror behind it in order to locate the leak.

Removing the growth
Brush the wall vigorously with a stiff-bristle brush. This can be an unpleasant, dusty job, so wear a facemask. Brush away from you to avoid debris being flicked into your eyes.

Microscopic spores will remain even after brushing. Kill these with a solution of bleach or, if the wall suffers from persistent fungal growth, use a proprietary fungicide, available from most DIY stores.

Using a bleach solution
Mix 1 part household bleach with 4 parts water and paint the solution on to the wall with an old paintbrush. Wash the surface with clean water, using a scrubbing brush, 48 hours later. Brush on a second application of bleach solution if the original fungal growth was severe.

Using a fungicidal solution
Dilute the fungicide with water according to the manufacturer's instructions and apply it liberally to the wall with an old paintbrush. Leave it for 24 hours, then rinse the wall with clean water. In extreme cases, give the wall two washes of fungicide, allowing 24 hours between applications and a further 24 hours before washing it down with water.

Removing efflorescence from masonry

Soluble salts within building materials such as cement, brick, stone and plaster gradually migrate to the surface along with the water as a wall dries out. The result is a white crystalline deposit called efflorescence.

The same condition can occur on old masonry if it is subjected to more than average moisture. Efflorescence itself is not harmful, but the source of the damp causing it must be identified and cured before decoration proceeds.

Regularly brush the deposit from the wall with a dry stiff-bristle brush or coarse sacking until the crystals cease to form. Do not attempt to wash off the crystals – they will merely dissolve in the water and soak back into the wall. Above all, do not attempt to decorate a wall which is still efflorescing, because this is a sign that it is still damp.

When the wall is completely dry, paint the surface with an alkali-resistant primer to neutralize the effect of the crystals before you apply an oil paint. Masonry paints and clear sealants that let the wall breathe are not affected by the alkali content of the masonry, so can be used without applying a primer.

PAINTING
EXTERIOR
MASONRY

SEE ALSO
Details for:
Cleaning masonry   25

Concrete floor paints

Floor paints are specially prepared to withstand hard wear. They are especially suitable for concrete garage or workshop floors, but they are also used for stone paving, steps and other concrete structures. They can be used inside for playroom floors.

The floor must be clean, dry and free from oil or grease. If the concrete is freshly laid, allow it to mature for at least a month before painting. Prime powdery or porous floors with a proprietary concrete sealer.

The best way to paint a large area is to use a paintbrush around the edges, then fit an extension to a paint roller for the bulk of the floor.

Apply paint with a roller on an extension

Paint in manageable sections
You can't hope to paint an entire house in one session, so divide each elevation into manageable sections to disguise the joins. The horizontal moulding divides the wall neatly into two sections, and the raised door and window surrounds are convenient break lines.

SUITABLE PAINTS FOR EXTERIOR MASONRY

There are various grades of paint suitable for decorating and protecting exterior masonry which take into account economy, standard of finish, durability and coverage. Use the chart opposite for quick reference.

Cement paint

Cement paint is supplied as a dry powder, to which water is added. It is based on white cement, but pigments are added to produce a range of colours. Cement paint is one of the cheaper paints suitable for exterior use. Spray new or porous surfaces with water before applying two coats.

Mixing cement paint
Shake or roll the container to loosen the powder, then add 2 volumes of powder to 1 of water in a clean bucket. Stir it to a smooth paste, then add a little more water until you achieve a full-bodied, creamy consistency. Mix up no more than you can use in one hour, or it will start to dry.

Adding an aggregate
When you are painting a dense wall or one treated with a stabilizing solution so that its porosity is substantially reduced, it is advisable to add clean sand to the mix to give it body. It also provides added protection for an exposed wall and helps to cover dark colours. If the sand changes the colour of the paint, add it to the first coat only. Use 1 part sand to 4 parts powder, stirring it in when the paint is still in its paste-like consistency.

Masonry paints

When buying weather-resistant exterior-masonry paints you have a choice between a smooth matt finish or a fine granular texture.

Water-based masonry paint
Most masonry paints are water-based, being in effect exterior-grade emulsions with additives that prevent mould growth. They are supplied ready for use, but in fact it pays to thin the first coat on porous walls with 20 per cent water. Follow up with one or two full-strength coats, depending on the colour of the paint.

Water-based masonry paints must be applied during fairly good weather. Damp or humid conditions and low temperatures may prevent the paint drying properly.

Solvent-based masonry paints
Some masonry paints are thinned with white spirit or with a special solvent, but unlike most oil paints they are moisture-vapour permeable so that the wall is able to breathe. It is often advisable to thin the first coat with 15 per cent white spirit, but check with the manufacturer's recommendations.

Solvent-based paints can be applied in practically any weather conditions, provided it is not actually raining.

Reinforced masonry paint
Masonry paint that has powdered mica or a similar fine aggregate added to it dries with a textured finish that is extremely weatherproof. Reinforced masonry paints are especially suitable in coastal districts and in industrial areas – where dark colours are also an advantage in that dirt will not show up so clearly as on a pale background. Although large cracks and holes must be filled prior to painting, reinforced masonry paint will cover hairline cracks and crazing.

Textured coating

A thick textured coating can be applied to exterior walls to form a thoroughly weatherproof, self-coloured coating which can also be overpainted to match other colours. The usual preparation is necessary and brickwork should be pointed flush. Large cracks should be filled, although a textured coating will cover fine cracks. The paste is brushed or rolled onto the wall, then left to harden, forming an even texture. However, if you prefer, you can produce a texture of your choice using a variety of simple tools. It is an easy process, but put in some practice on a small section first.

WALLS
MORTAR

MORTAR
FOR MASONRY
WALLS

SEE ALSO

In the building of a wall, mortar is employed to bind together the bricks, concrete blocks or stones. The durability of a masonry wall depends upon the quality of the mortar used in its construction. If it is mixed correctly to the right consistency the mortar will become strong yet flexible, but if the ingredients are added in the wrong proportions it may be weak or, conversely, so hard that it is prone to cracking. If too much water is added to the mix the mortar will be squeezed out of the joints by the weight of the masonry, while if the mortar is too dry adhesion will be poor.

BRICKLAYERS' TERMS

Bricklayers use a number of specialized words and phrases to describe their craft and materials. Terms used frequently are listed below while others are described as they occur.

BRICK FACES *The surfaces of a brick.*
Stretcher faces *The long sides of a brick.*
Header faces *The short ends of a brick.*
Bedding faces *The top and bottom surfaces.*
Frog *The depression in one bedding face.*

COURSES *The individual, horizontal rows of bricks.*
Stretcher course *A single course with stretcher faces visible.*
Header course *A single course with header faces visible.*
Coping *The top course designed to protect the wall from rainwater.*
Bond *Pattern produced by staggering alternate courses so that vertical joints are not aligned one above the other.*
Stretcher *A single brick from a stretcher course.*
Header *A single brick from a header course.*
Closure brick *The last brick laid in a course.*

CUT BRICKS *Bricks cut with a bolster chisel to even up the bond.*
Bat *A brick cut across its width, i.e. half-bat, three-quarter bat.*
Queen closer *A brick cut along its length.*

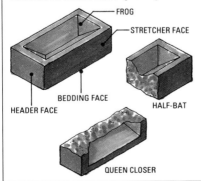

FROG
STRETCHER FACE
BEDDING FACE
HEADER FACE
HALF-BAT
QUEEN CLOSER

The ingredients of mortar

The ingredients of general-purpose mortar are cement, hydrated lime and sand, mixed with enough water to make a workable paste.

Cement is the hardening agent which binds the other ingredients together. The lime slows down the drying process and prevents the mortar setting too quickly. It also makes the mix flow well so that it fills gaps in the masonry and adheres to the texture of blocks or bricks. The sand acts as fine aggregate, adding body to the mortar, and reduces the possibility of shrinkage.

Use fine builders' sand for general-purpose mortar; if you want a paler mortar to bond white screen blocks, use silver sand.

Mixing mortar

Mortar must be used within two hours of mixing or discarded, so make only as much as you can use within that time. An average of about two minutes to lay one brick is a reasonable estimate.

Choose a flat site upon which to mix the materials – a sheet of plywood will do – and dampen it slightly to prevent it absorbing water from the mortar. Make a pile of half the amount of sand to be used, then add the other ingredients. Put the rest of the sand on top, and mix the dry materials thoroughly.

Scoop a depression in the pile and add clean tap water. Never use contaminated or salty water. Push the dry mix from around the edge of the pile into the water until it has absorbed enough for you to blend the mix with a shovel, using a chopping action. Add more water, little by little, until the mortar has a butter-like consistency, slipping easily from the shovel but firm enough to hold its shape if you make a hollow in the mix. If the sides of the hollow collapse, add more dry ingredients until the mortar firms up. Make sure the mortar is sufficiently moist; dry mortar won't form a strong bond with the masonry.

If mortar stiffens up while you are working, add just enough water to restore the consistency and dampen the mixing board again.

Proportions for masonry mixes

Mix the ingredients according to the prevailing conditions at the building site. Use a general-purpose mortar for moderate conditions where the wall is reasonably sheltered and a stronger mix for severe conditions where the wall will be exposed to wind and driving rain, or where the site is elevated or near the coast. If you are using plasticizer rather than lime, follow the manufacturer's instructions regarding the quantity you should add to the sand.

Plasticizers
If you are laying masonry in a period of cold weather, substitute a proprietary plasticizer for the lime. Plasticizer produces aerated mortar in which the tiny air bubbles allow water to expand in freezing conditions, so reducing the risk of cracking. Premixed masonry cement, which has an aerating agent, is ready for mixing with sand.

Ready-mix mortar
Ready-mix mortar contains all the essential ingredients mixed to the correct proportions; you simply add water. It is a more expensive way of buying mortar but is convenient to use and available in small quantities.

Correct consistency
The mortar mix should be firm enough to hold its shape when you make a depression in the mix.

● **Estimating quantity**
As a rough guide to estimating how much mortar you will need when building single-skin walls, allow approximately 1cu m (1⅓ cu yd) of sand (other ingredients in proportion) to lay: 3364 bricks; 1946 average concrete blocks; and 1639 decorative screen blocks.

● **Masonry cement**
A ready-mixed cement that is used without adding lime or plasticizer.

MORTAR MIXING PROPORTIONS	Cement/lime mortar	Plasticized mortar	Masonry cement mortar
General-purpose mortar (Moderate conditions)	1 part cement 1 part lime 6 parts sand	1 part cement 6 parts sand/ plasticizer	1 part cement 5 parts sand
Strong mortar (Severe conditions)	1 part cement ½ part lime 4 parts sand	1 part cement 4 parts sand/ plasticizer	1 part cement 3 parts sand

27

BONDING
BRICKWORK

DESIGNING A WALL FOR STABILITY

It is easy enough to appreciate the loads and stresses imposed upon the walls of a house or outbuilding, and therefore the necessity for solid foundations and adequate methods of reinforcement and protection to prevent them collapsing. It is not so obvious that even simple garden walling requires similar measures to ensure its stability. It is merely irritating if a low dividing wall or planter falls apart, but a serious injury could result from the collapse of a heavy boundary wall.

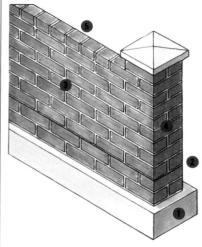

The basic structure of a wall
Unless you design and build a wall in the correct manner, it will not be strong and stable.

1 Footings
A wall must be built upon a solid concrete platform known as a strip footing. The dimensions of the footing vary according to the height and weight of the wall.

2 Damp-proof course
A layer of waterproof material 150mm (6in) above ground level stops water rising from the soil. It is not needed for most garden walling unless it abuts a building with a similar DPC. Not only does it protect the house from damp, but it reduces the likelihood of freezing water expanding and cracking the joints.

3 Bonding
The staggered pattern of bricks is not merely decorative. It is designed to spread the static load along the wall and to tie the individual units together.

4 Piers
Straight walls over a certain height and length must be buttressed at regular intervals with thick columns of brickwork known as piers. They resist the sideways pressure caused by high winds.

5 Coping
The coping prevents frost damage by shedding rainwater from the top of the wall where it could seep into the upper brick joints.

Mortar is extremely strong under compression, but its tensile strength is relatively weak. If bricks were stacked one upon the other so that the vertical joints were continuous, any movement within the wall would pull them apart and the structure would be seriously weakened. Bonding brickwork staggers the vertical joints, transmitting the load along the entire length of the wall. Try out the bond of your choice first by dry-laying just a few bricks before you embark upon the building work.

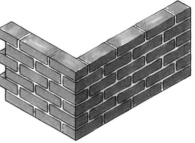

Stretcher bond
The stretcher bond is the simplest form of bonding and is used for single-thickness walls, including the two individual leaves of a cavity wall found in the construction of modern buildings. Half-bats are used to make the bond at the end of a straight wall, while a corner is formed by alternating headers and stretchers.

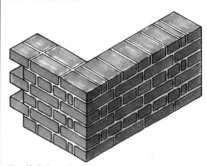

English bond
If you were to build a 215mm (8½in) thick wall by laying courses of stretcher-bonded bricks side by side, there would be a weak vertical joint running centrally down the wall. An English bond strengthens the wall by using alternate courses of headers. Staggered joints are maintained at the end of a wall and at a right-angle corner by inserting a queen closer before the last header.

Flemish bond
The Flemish bond is another method used for building a solid, 215mm (8½in) thick wall. Every course is laid with alternate headers and stretchers. Stagger the joint at the end of a course and at a corner by laying a queen closer before the header.

Decorative bonds
Stretcher, English and Flemish bonds are designed to construct strong walls – decorative qualities are incidental. Other bonds, used primarily for their visual effect, are suitable for low, non-loadbearing walls only, supported by a conventionally bonded base and piers.

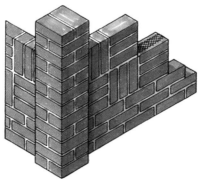

Stack bonding A basket-weave effect is achieved by stack-bonding bricks in groups of three. Strengthen the continuous vertical joints with wall ties.

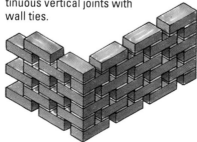

Honeycomb bond Build an open, decorative screen using a stretcher-like bond with a quarter-bat-size space between each brick. Build the screen carefully to keep the bond regular, and cut quarter-bats to fill the gaps in the top course.

CONSTRUCTING STRIP FOOTINGS

Stringent Building Regulations govern the size and reinforcement required for the footings to support high walls (and especially those that are structural). However, the majority of garden walls can be built upon concrete footings laid in a straight-sided trench.

Size of footings

The footing must be sufficiently substantial to support the weight of the wall, and the soil must be firm and well-drained to avoid possible subsidence. It is unwise to set footings in ground which has been filled recently, such as a new building site. Take care also to avoid tree roots and drainpipes. If the trench begins to fill with water as you are digging, seek professional advice before proceeding.

Dig the trench deeper than the footing itself so that the first one or two courses of brick are below ground level. This will allow for an adequate depth of soil for planting right up to the wall.

If the soil is not firmly packed when you reach the required depth, dig deeper until you reach a firm level, then fill the bottom of the trench with compacted hardcore up to the lowest level of the proposed footing.

SLOPING-SITE FOOTINGS

When the ground slopes gently, simply ignore the gradient and make the footing perfectly level. If the site slopes noticeably, make a stepped footing by placing plywood shuttering across the trench at regular intervals. Calculate the height and length of the steps using multiples of normal brick size.

SEE ALSO
Details for:
Concrete mixes 43
Mixing concrete 44

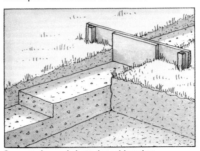
Support plywood shuttering with stakes

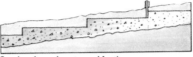
Section through a stepped footing
A typical stepped concrete footing with one of the plywood shuttering boards in place.

RECOMMENDED DIMENSIONS FOR FOOTINGS

Type of wall	Height of wall	Thickness of footing	Width of footing
One brick thick	Up to 1m (3ft 3in)	150mm (6in)	300mm (1ft)
Two bricks thick	Up to 1m (3ft 3in)	225 to 300mm (9in to 1ft)	450mm (1ft 6in)
Two bricks thick	Over 1m up to 2m (Up to 6ft 6in)	375 to 450mm (1ft 3in to 1ft 6in)	450 to 600mm (1ft 6in to 2ft)
Retaining wall	Up to 1m (3ft 3in)	150 to 300mm (6in to 1ft)	375 to 450mm (1ft 3in to 1ft 6in)

Setting out the footings

For a straight footing, set up two profile boards made from 25mm (1in) thick timber nailed to stakes driven into the ground at each end of the proposed trench, but well outside the work area.

Drive nails into the top edge of each board and stretch lines between them to mark the front and back edges of the wall. Then drive nails into the boards on each side of the wall line to indicate the width of the footing and stretch more lines between them (1). When you are satisfied the setting out is accurate, remove the lines marking the wall but leave the nails so you can replace the lines when you come to lay the bricks.

Place a spirit level against the remaining lines to mark the edge of the footing on the ground (2). Mark the ends of the footing extending beyond the line of the wall by half the wall's thickness. Mark the edge of the trench on the ground with a spade and remove the lines. Leave the boards in place.

Turning corners

If your wall will have a right-angled corner, set up two sets of profile boards as before, checking carefully that the lines form a true right angle using the 3 : 4 : 5 principle (3).

Digging the trench

Excavate the trench, keeping the sides vertical, and check that the bottom is level, using a long, straight piece of wood and a spirit level.

Drive a stake into the bottom of the trench near one end until the top of the stake represents the depth of the footing. Drive in more stakes at about 1m (3ft) intervals, checking that the tops are level (4).

Filling the trench

Pour a foundation mix of concrete (see MIXING CONCRETE BY VOLUME) into the trench, then tamp it down firmly with a stout piece of timber until it is exactly level with the top of the stakes. Leave the stakes in place and allow the footing to harden thoroughly before building the wall.

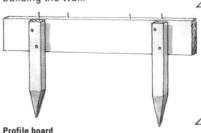
Profile board

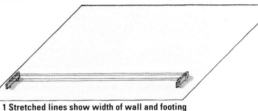
1 Stretched lines show width of wall and footing

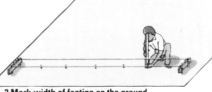
2 Mark width of footing on the ground

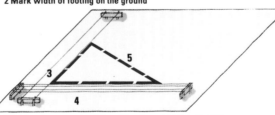
3 A triangle measuring 3, 4 and 5 units makes a right angle

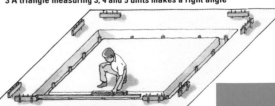
4 Check the tops of the stakes are level

LAYING BRICKS

BRICKLAYING TOOLS

While you can improvise a number of builder's tools, you will have to buy some of the more specialized tools that are used by bricklayers.

Tools for basic bricklaying
1 Club hammer 2 Spirit level 3 Bolster chisel
4 Pointing trowel 5 Brick trowel

Spreading a bed of mortar – throwing a line – requires practice before you can develop speed, so concentrate at first on laying bricks accurately. Mixing the mortar to exactly the right consistency helps to keep the visible faces of the bricks clean. In hot, dry weather dampen the footings and bricks, but let any surface water evaporate before you lay the bricks.

Bricklaying techniques

Hold the brick trowel with your thumb in line with the handle, pointing towards the tip of the blade (**1**).

Scoop a measure of mortar out of the pile and shape it roughly to match the dimensions of the trowel blade. Pick up the mortar by sliding the blade under the pile, setting it onto the trowel with a slight jerk of the wrist (**2**).

Spread the mortar along the top course by aligning the edge of the trowel with the centre line of the bricks. As you tip the blade to deposit the mortar, draw the trowel back towards you to stretch the bed over at least two to three bricks (**3**). Furrow the mortar by pressing the point of the trowel along the centre (**4**).

Pick up a brick with your other hand, but don't extend your thumb too far onto the stretcher face or it will disturb the builders' line (see right) every time you place a brick in position. Press the brick into the bed, picking up excess mortar squeezed from the joint by sliding the edge of the trowel along the wall (**5**).

With the mortar picked up on the trowel, butter the header of the next brick, making a neat 10mm (⅜in) bed for the header joint (**6**). Press the brick against its neighbour, scooping off excess mortar with the trowel.

Having laid three bricks, use a spirit level to check that they are horizontal. Make any adjustments by tapping them down with the trowel handle (**7**).

Hold the spirit level along the outer edge of the bricks to check that they are in line. To move a brick sideways without knocking it off its mortar bed, tap the upper edge with the trowel at about 45 degrees (**8**).

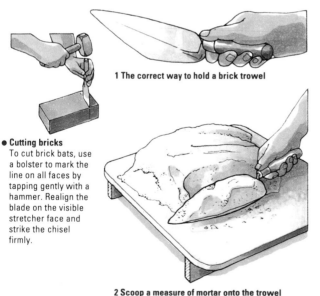

1 The correct way to hold a brick trowel

● **Cutting bricks**
To cut brick bats, use a bolster to mark the line on all faces by tapping gently with a hammer. Realign the blade on the visible stretcher face and strike the chisel firmly.

2 Scoop a measure of mortar onto the trowel

3 Stretch a bed of mortar along the course

4 Furrow the mortar with the trowel point

5 Push down brick and remove excess mortar

6 Butter the head of the next brick

7 Level the course of bricks with the trowel

8 Tap the bricks sideways to align them

BUILDING A STRETCHER-BONDED WALL

A single-width brick wall tends to look visually mean and, over a certain height, is also structurally weak unless it is supported with piers, or changes direction by forming right-angle corners. The ability to construct accurate right-angle corners is a requirement for building most structures, even simple garden planters. The main thing to remember is to keep checking and rechecking the alignment of the bricks.

Setting out the corners

Mark out the footings and face of the wall by stretching string lines between profile boards. When the footings have been filled and the concrete has set, use a plumb line or hold a level lightly against the line to mark the corners and the face of the wall on the footing (1). Join the marks with a pencil and straight batten, and check the accuracy of the corners with a builder's square. Stretch a line between the corner marks to check the alignment.

Building the corners

Build the corners first as a series of steps or 'leads' before filling between. It is essential that they form true right angles, so take your time.

Throw a bed of mortar, then lay three bricks in both directions against the marked line. Make sure that they are level in all directions, checking the diagonal by laying a spirit level between the end bricks (2).

Build the leads to a height of five stepped courses, using a gauge stick to measure the height of each course as you proceed (3). Use alternate headers and stretchers to form the actual point of the corner.

Use a level to plumb the corner, and check the alignment of the stepped bricks by holding the level against the side of the wall (4).

A stepped lead for a corner

2 Level the first course of bricks

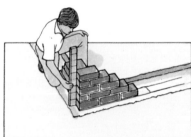
3 Check the height with a gauge stick

1 Mark the face of the wall on the footing

4 Check that the steps are in line

Building the straight sections

Stretch a builder's line between the corners so that it aligns perfectly with the top of the first course (5).

Lay the first straight course of bricks from both ends towards the middle. As you near the middle point, lay the last few bricks dry to make certain they will fit. If necessary, cut the central or 'closure' brick to fit. Mortar the bricks in place, finishing with the closure brick by spreading mortar onto both ends and onto the header faces of the bricks on each side (6). Scoop off excess mortar with the trowel.

Lay subsequent courses between the leads in the same way, raising the builder's line each time. To build the wall higher, raise the corners first by constructing leads to the required height, then fill the spaces between.

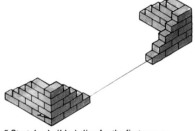
5 Stretch a builder's line for the first course

6 Carefully lay the last or closure brick

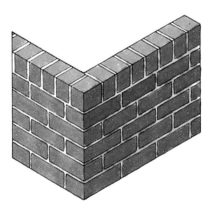
Coping the wall
You could finish the wall by laying the last course frog downwards, but a coping of half-bats laid on end looks more professional. Alternatively, use proprietary coping bricks or blocks.

● **Covering the wall**
Cover finished or partly built walls overnight with sheets of polyethylene or tarpaulin to protect the brickwork from rain or frost. Weight the edges of the covers with bricks.

● **Building a straight wall**
To build a straight wall without a corner, follow the procedure described left, building end leads – straight stepped sections – at each end of the wall, then fill between with bricks.

31

POINTING BRICKWORK

Pointing the mortar joints makes for a packed, watertight joint as well as enhancing the appearance of the wall. Well-struck joints and clean brickwork are essential if the wall is to look professionally built; for best results, the mortar must be shaped when it is just the right consistency.

The consistency of the mortar

If the mortar is still too wet the joint will not be crisp and you may drag mortar out from between the bricks. On the other hand, if it is left to harden too long, pointing will be hard work and you may leave dark marks on the joint.

Test the consistency of the mortar by pressing your thumb into a joint. If it holds a clear impression without sticking to your thumb the mortar is just right for pointing. Because it is so important that you shape the joint at exactly the right moment you may have to point the work in stages before you can complete the wall. Shape the joints to match existing brickwork or choose a profile that is suitable for the prevailing weather conditions.

How to make pointing joints

Flush joint

Rubbed joint

V-joint

Raked joint

Weatherstruck joint

● **Coloured mortar**
You can add coloured powders to your mortar mix. Make a trial batch to test the colour when dry. Rake out the joint and apply it carefully to avoid staining the bricks.

Flush joint
Having scraped the mortar flush with the edge of the trowel, stipple the joints with a stiff-bristle brush to expose the sand aggregate.

Rubbed (concave) joint
Buy a shaped jointing tool to make a rubbed joint, or improvise with a length of bent tubing. Flush the mortar first, then drag the tool along the joints. Finish the vertical joints, then do the horizontal ones. This is a utilitarian joint, ideal for a wall built with second-hand bricks which are not of a sufficiently good quality to take a crisp joint.

Shape the mortar with a jointing tool

V-joint
Produced in a similar way to the rubbed joint, the V-joint gives a very smart finish to new brickwork and sheds rainwater well.

Raked joint
Use a piece of wood or metal to rake out the joints to a depth of about 6mm (¼in), then compress them again by smoothing the mortar lightly with a lath or piece of rounded dowel rod. Raked joints do not shed water, so they are not suitable for an exposed site.

Weatherstruck joint
The angled weatherstruck joint is ideal, even in harsh conditions. Use a small pointing trowel to shape the vertical joints **(1)**. They can slope to the left or right, but be consistent throughout the same section of brickwork. Shape the horizontal joints allowing the mortar to spill out slightly at the base of each joint. Professionals finish the joint by cutting off excess mortar with a tool called a Frenchman, similar to a table knife but with the tip at 90 degrees. Improvise a similar tool with a strip of bent metal. Nail two scraps of plywood to a batten to hold it away from the wall. Align the batten with the bottom of the joint to guide the tool and make a neat, straight edge to the mortar **(2)**.

1 Shape a weatherstruck joint with a trowel

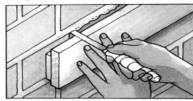

2 Remove excess mortar with a Frenchman

Brushing the brickwork
Let the shaped joints harden a little before you clean scraps of mortar from the face of the wall. Use a medium-soft banister brush, sweeping lightly across the joints so as not to damage them.

COPING FOR BRICK WALLS

The coping which forms the top course of the wall protects the brickwork from weathering and gives the wall a finished appearance. Strictly speaking, if the coping is flush with both faces of the wall it is called a capping; a true coping projects from the face so that water drips clear and does not leave a stain on the brickwork.

You can lay a coping of bricks with their stretcher faces across the width of the wall. Use the same type of brick as that employed in the construction of the wall, or engineering bricks – the water-resistant quality of the latter is an advantage and the colour contrasts pleasingly with regular brickwork. You can also obtain special coping bricks designed to shed rainwater

Stone or cast-concrete slabs are popular for garden walling. They are quick to lay and are wide enough to form low, bench-type seating.

On an exposed site, consider installing a damp-proof course under the coping to reduce the risk of frost attack. Use a standard bituminous-felt DPC or lay two courses of plain roof tiles with staggered joints and a brick coping above. Let the tiles project from the face of the wall, but run a sloping mortar joint along the top of the projection to shed water.

Brick coping
Specially shaped bricks are designed to shed rainwater.

Slab coping
Choose a concrete or stone slab that is wider than the wall itself.

Tile-and-brick coping
Lay flat roof tiles or specially made creasing tiles beneath a brick coping to form a weatherproof layer which allows water to drip clear of the wall.

When building new garden walls which intersect at right angles, either anchor them by bonding the brickwork (see below) or take the easier option and link them with wall ties at every third course. If the intersecting wall is over 2m (6ft 6in) in length, make the junction a control joint by using straight metal strips as wall ties.

Stretcher bond

English bond

Flemish bond

Using a wall tie

BUILDING INTERSECTING WALLS

Building up to an existing wall

When you build a new wall to intersect with the existing wall of a house you must include a damp-proof course to prevent water bridging the house DPC via the new masonry. You must also make a positive joint between the walls.

Inserting a DPC
Building Regulations require a damp-proof course in all habitable buildings to prevent rising damp. This consists of a layer of impervious material built into the mortar bed 150mm (6in) above ground level. When you build a new wall, its DPC must coincide with the DPC in the existing structure. Use a roll of bituminous felt chosen to match the thickness of the new wall.

Locate the house DPC and build the first few courses of the new wall up to that level. Spread a thin bed of mortar on the bricks and lay the DPC upon it with the end of the roll turned up against the existing wall (1). The next course of bricks will trap the DPC between the header joint and the wall. Lay more mortar on top of the DPC to produce the standard 10mm (⅜in) joint ready for laying the next course in the normal way. If you have to join rolls of DPC, overlap the ends by 150mm (6in).

Tying-in the new wall
The traditional method for linking a new wall with an existing structure involves chopping recesses in the brickwork at every fourth course. End bricks of the new wall are set into the recesses, bonding the two structures together (2). An alternative and much simpler method, however, is to screw to the wall a special stainless-metal channel which is designed to accept bricks or concrete blocks and provide anchoring points for standard wire wall ties. Channels are available for masonry units up to 215mm (8½in) thick.

Screw the channel to the old wall above the DPC with stainless-steel coachscrews and wall plugs, or use expanding bolts (3). While it is not essential, it is advisable to trap 1m (3ft 3in) of DPC felt behind the channel.

Mortar the end of a brick before feeding it into the channel (4). As the brick is pushed home, the mortar squeezes through the perforated channel to make a firm bond.

At every third course, hook a wall tie over the pressed lugs in the channel and bed it firmly into the mortar joint (5).

1 Lap the existing DPC with the new roll

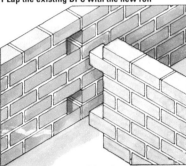
2 You can tooth the wall into the brickwork

3 But it is easier to use a special channel

4 Locate the ends of the bricks in the channel

5 Hook wire wall ties over the pressed lugs

DPC on a sloping site
When the site slopes noticeably, the wall footing is stepped to keep the top of the wall level. If you include a DPC in the wall, that too must follow the line of the steps to keep it the required height above ground level.

33

BRICKWORK
PIERS

A pier is, strictly speaking, a freestanding column of masonry which may be used, for example, as a support for a porch or a pergola or as an individual gatepost. When a column is built as part of a wall, it is more accurately termed a pilaster. In practice, however, the word 'column' is often used to cover either description. To avoid confusion, any supporting brick column will be described here as a pier. Thorough planning is essential when building piers.

Structural considerations

Any freestanding straight wall over a certain length and height must be buttressed at regular intervals by piers. Sections of walling and piers must be tied together, either by a brick bond or by inserting metal wall ties in every third course of bricks. Any single-width brick wall, whatever its height, would benefit from supporting piers at open ends and gateways where it is most vulnerable; these will also improve the appearance of the wall. Piers over 1m (3ft 3in), and especially those supporting gates, should be built around steel reinforcing rods set in the concrete footings. Whether reinforcing is included or not, allow for the size of piers when designing the footings.

Designing the piers

Piers should be placed no more than 3m (9ft 9in) apart in walls over a certain height (see the chart below). The wall itself can be flush with one face of a pier, but the structure is stronger if it is centred on the pier.

Piers should be a minimum of twice the thickness of a 102.5mm (4in) thick wall, but build 328mm (1ft 1½in) square piers when reinforcement is required, such as for gateways, and to buttress 215mm (8½in) thick walls.

INCORPORATING PIERS IN A BRICK WALL		
Thickness of wall	Maximum height without piers	Maximum pier spacing
102.5mm (4in)	450mm (1ft 6in)	3m (9ft 9in)
215mm (8½)	1.35m (4ft 6in)	3m (9ft 9in)

BONDING PIERS

If you prefer the appearance of bonded-brick piers, construct them as shown below. It is easier, however, to use wall ties to reinforce continuous vertical joints in the brickwork, especially when building walls centred on piers.

Various types of galvanized-metal wall ties are available: wire bent into a butterfly shape (1); stamped-metal steel strips with forked ends, known as fish tails (2); and expanded-metal mesh cut in straight strips (3).

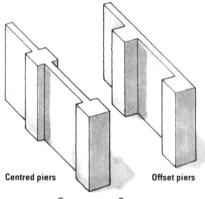

Centred piers   **Offset piers**

Bonding piers
While it is simpler to tie a wall to a pier with wall ties (see above right), it is relatively easy to bond a pier into a wall that is of single-brick width.

Colour key
You will have to cut certain bricks to bond a pier into a straight wall. Whole bricks are coloured with a light tone, three-quarter bats with a medium tone, and half-bats with a dark tone.

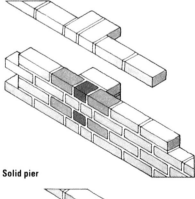

Solid pier

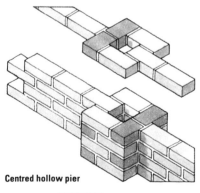

Centred hollow pier

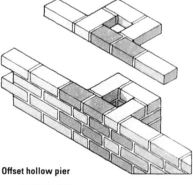

Offset hollow pier

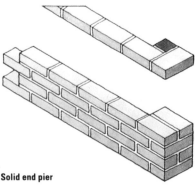

Solid end pier

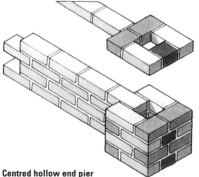

Centred hollow end pier

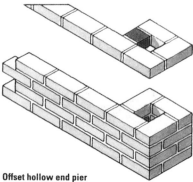

Offset hollow end pier

BUILDING
PIERS

Mark out accurately the positions of piers and the face of the wall on the concrete footing. Lay the first course for the piers using a builder's line stretched between two stakes to align them **(1)**. Adjust the position of the line if necessary and fill in between with the first straight course, working from both ends towards the middle **(2)**. Build alternate pier and wall courses, checking the level and the vertical faces and corners of the piers. At the third course, push metal wall ties into the mortar bed to span the joint between wall and pier **(3)**. Continue in the same way to the required height of the wall, then raise the piers to their required height **(4)**. Lay a coping along the wall and cap the piers with concrete or stone slabs **(5)**.

1 Lay pier bases
Stretch a builder's line to position the bases of the piers.

2 Lay first wall course
Use the line to keep the first course straight.

3 Lay pier ties
Join the piers to the wall by inserting wall ties into every third course. Put a tie into alternate courses for a gate-supporting pier.

4 Raise the piers
Build the piers higher than the wall to allow for a decorative coping along the top course.

5 Lay the coping
Lay coping slabs and cap the piers.

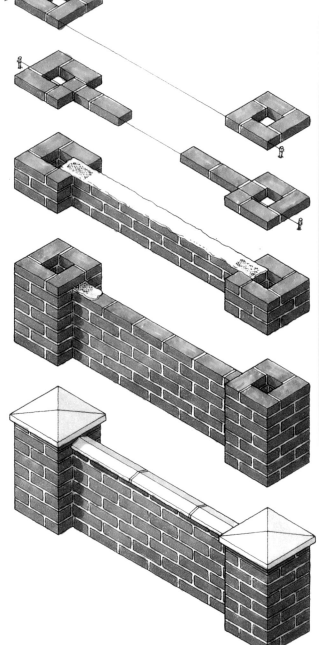

Incorporating control joints

Although it is not noticeable, a brick wall moves constantly as a result of ground settlement as well as expansion and contraction of the materials. Over short distances the movement is so slight that it has hardly any effect on the brickwork, but in a long wall it can crack the structure. To compensate for this movement, build unmortared, continuous vertical joints into a wall at intervals of about 6m (19ft 6in). Although these control joints can be placed in a straight section of walling, it is neater and more convenient to place them where the wall meets a pier. Build the pier and wall as normal, but omit the mortar from the header joints of the wall. Instead of inserting standard wall ties, embed a flat, 3mm (⅛in) thick galvanized strip in the mortar bed. Lightly grease one half of the strip with motor grease or petroleum jelly so that it can slide lengthwise to allow for movement yet still key the wall and pier together. When the wall is complete, fill the joint from both sides with mastic.

Adding reinforcement

Use 16mm (⅝in) steel reinforcing bars to strengthen brick piers. If the pier is under 1m (3ft 3in) in height, use one continuous length of bar **(1)**; for taller piers, embed a bent 'starter' bar in the footing, projecting a minimum of 500mm (1ft 8in) above the level of the concrete **(2)**. As the work proceeds, use galvanized wire to bind extension bars to the projection of the starter bar up to within 50mm (2in) of the top of the pier. Fill in around the reinforcement with concrete as you build the pier, but pack it very carefully so that you do not disturb the brickwork.

Making a control joint
Tie the pier to the wall with galvanized-metal strips when making a control joint (shown here before it is set in mortar). The mastic is squeezed into the joint between the wall and the pier.

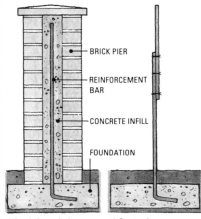

BRICK PIER

REINFORCEMENT BAR

CONCRETE INFILL

FOUNDATION

1 A reinforced pier   **2 Starter bar**

BUILDING WITH CONCRETE BLOCKS

● **Building piers**
High, free-standing garden walls constructed from blocks must be supported by piers at 3m (9ft 9in) intervals.

The methods for laying concrete blocks are much the same as for building with bricks. Block walls need similar concrete footings and the same type of mortar, although heavy blocks should be laid with a firm mix to resist the additional weight of the freshly constructed wall. As blocks are made in a greater variety of sizes, you can build a wall of any thickness with a simple stretcher bond. However, don't dampen concrete blocks before laying them – wet blocks can shrink and crack the mortar joints as the wall dries out. When you are building decorative walls with facing blocks use any of the pointing styles described for bricks, but flush-joint a wall built with structural blocks which is to be rendered or plastered by rubbing the joints with sacking.

CONTROL JOINTS

Walls over 6m (19ft 6in) long should be built with a continuous vertical control joint to allow for expansion. Place an unmortared joint in a straight section of wall or against a pier, and bridge the gap with galvanized-metal dowels as for brickwork. Fill the gap with mastic.

If you need to insert a control joint in a dividing wall, form the joint between the doorframe and wall. Fill the joints with mortar in the normal way, but rake them out to a depth of 18mm (¾in) round one end of the lintel and vertically to the ceiling on both sides of the wall. Fill the control joint flush with mastic.

Forming a control joint next to a door opening
Take the joint around the lintel and up to the ceiling on both sides of the wall.

Building a dividing wall

Building a non-loadbearing stud partition is the usual method employed for dividing up a large internal space into smaller rooms, but if your house is built on a concrete pad, a practical alternative is to use concrete blocks. If you install a doorway in the dividing wall, plan its position to avoid cutting away too many blocks. Allow for the wooden doorframe and lining as well as a precast lintel to support the masonry above the opening. Fill the space above the lintel with cut blocks or bricks to level the courses.

Screw galvanized pressed-metal channels to the existing structure to support each end of the dividing wall. Plumb them accurately or the new wall will be out of true. Lay the first course of blocks without mortar across the room to check their spacing and the position of a doorway if it is to be included. Mark the positions of the blocks before building stepped leads at each end as for brickwork. Check for accuracy with a spirit level, then fill in between the leads with blocks.

Build another three courses of blocks, anchoring the end blocks to the channels with wall ties in every joint. Leave the mortar to harden overnight before you continue with the wall.

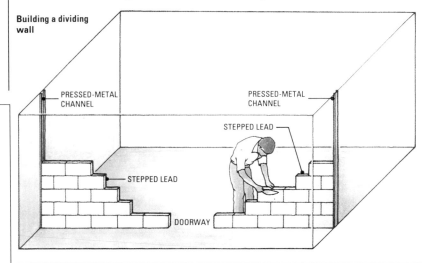

Building a dividing wall

PRESSED-METAL CHANNEL

PRESSED-METAL CHANNEL

STEPPED LEAD

STEPPED LEAD

DOORWAY

Building intersecting walls

Butt intersecting garden walls together with a continuous vertical joint between them, but anchor the structure as for brickwork with wire-mesh wall ties (**1**). If you build a wall with heavyweight hollow blocks, use stout metal tie bars with a bend at each end. Fill the block cores with mortar to embed the ends of the bars (**2**). Install a tie in every course.

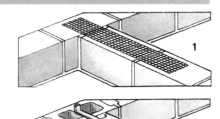

1 Wire-mesh wall ties for solid blocks ▶
2 Metal tie bar for hollow blocks

Cutting blocks

To cut a concrete block, use a bolster chisel and straightedge to score a line right round it. Deepen the line into a groove by striking the chisel sharply with a club hammer, working your way round the face of the concrete block until it eventually fractures along the chiselled groove.

Cutting a block
Use a bolster and club hammer to cut a block.

Basic bricklaying techniques and tools are used to build a pierced concrete screen, but because the blocks are stack-bonded – with continuous vertical joints – the wall must be reinforced vertically with 16mm (⅝in) steel bars, and horizontally with galvanized mesh if it is built higher than 600mm (2ft). Build the screen with supporting piers no more than 3m (9ft 9in) apart, using matching pilaster blocks. Alternatively, if you prefer the appearance of contrasting masonry, construct a base and piers from bricks or facing blocks.

Constructing the screen

Set out and fill the footings twice the width of the pilaster blocks. Embed pier-reinforcing bars in the concrete and support them with guy ropes until the concrete sets.

Lower a pilaster block over the first bar, setting it onto a bed of mortar laid around the base of the bar. Check the block is perfectly vertical and level, and that its locating channel faces the next pier. Pack mortar or concrete into its core, then proceed with two more blocks so that the pier corresponds to the height of two mortared screen blocks (1). Construct each pier in the same way. Intermediate piers will have a locating channel on each side.

Allow the mortar to harden overnight, then lay a mortar bed for two screen blocks next to the first pier. Butter the vertical edge of a screen block and press it into the pier locating channel. Tap it into the mortar bed and check it is level. Mortar the next block

and place it alongside the first. When buttering screen blocks, take special care to keep the faces clean by making a neat, chamfered bed of mortar on each block (3).

Lay two more blocks against the next pier, stretch a builder's line to gauge the top edge of the first course, then lay the rest of the blocks towards the centre, making sure the vertical joints are aligned perfectly. Before building any higher, embed a wire reinforcing strip running from pier to pier in the next mortar bed (4). Continue to build the piers and screen up to a maximum height of 2m (6ft 6in), inserting a wire strip into alternate courses. Finally, lay coping slabs on top of each pier and along the top of the screen (5).

If you don't like the appearance of ordinary mortar joints, rake out some of the mortar and repoint with mortar made with silver sand. A concave rubbed joint suits decorative screening.

1 Build the piers

2 Fit block to pier

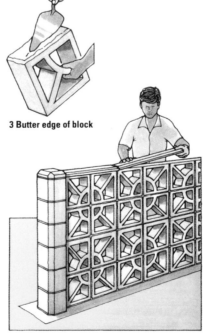

3 Butter edge of block

4 Lay a wire reinforcing strip into the mortar

5 Lay coping slabs along the wall

CAVITY WALLS

Cavity walls are used in the construction of habitable buildings to prevent the passage of moisture through the wall to the interior. This is achieved by building two independent leaves of masonry with a clear gap between them. The gap provides a degree of thermal insulation, but the insulation value increases appreciably if an efficient insulant is introduced to the cavity. The exterior leaf of most cavity walls is constructed with facing bricks. The inner leaf is sometimes built with interior-grade bricks, but more often with concrete blocks. Whatever type of masonry is used, both leaves must be tied together with wall ties spanning the gap. Cavity walls are likely to be loadbearing, so have to be built very accurately – hire a professional for this job. Make sure he or she includes a DPC in both leaves and avoids dropping mortar into the gap; if mortar collects at the base of the cavity, or even on one of the wall ties, moisture can bridge the gap and cause damp on the inside.

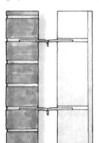

Cavity-wall construction
A section through a typical cavity wall built with an exterior leaf of bricks tied to an inner leaf of plastered concrete blocks.

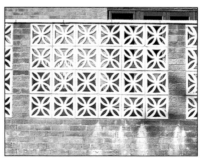

Building a brick base and piers
You can construct a wall using a combination of bricks and screen blocks. Build a low base of bricks with reinforced piers spaced so as to accord with the size of the blocks. Build up the piers and the screen blocks together and tie them with reinforcing strips as described left, inserting standard wall ties in alternate courses to provide additional location and support.

BUILDING WITH STONE

Constructing garden walling with natural stone requires a different approach to that needed for bricklaying or building with concrete blocks. A stone wall must be as stable as one built with any other masonry, but its visual appeal relies on the coursing being less regular; indeed, there is no real coursing when a wall is built with undressed stone or rubble.

Structural considerations

Stone walls don't necessarily require mortar to hold the stones together, although it is often used, especially with dressed or semi-dressed stone, to provide additional stability. As a result, many stone walls taper, having a wide base of heavy, flat stones and gradually decreasing in width as the wall rises.

This traditional form of construction was developed to prevent a wall of unmortared stones toppling sideways when subjected to high winds or the weight of farm animals. Far from detracting from its appearance, this informal construction suits a country-style garden perfectly.

Building a dry-stone wall

A true dry-stone wall is built without mortar, relying instead on a selective choice of stones and careful placement to provide stability. Experience is needed for perfect results, but there is no reason why you cannot introduce mortar, particularly within the core of the wall, and still maintain the appearance of dry-stone walling. You can also bed the stones in soil, packing it firmly into the crevices as you lay each course. This enables you to plant alpines or other suitable rockery plants in the wall, even during construction.

When you select the masonry, look out for flat stones in a variety of sizes and make sure you have some large enough to run the full width of the wall, especially at the base of the structure. These 'bonding' stones, placed at regular intervals, are important components which tie the loose rubble into a cohesive structure. Even a low wall will inevitably include some heavy stones. When you lift them, keep your back straight and your feet together, using the strong muscles of your legs to take the strain.

DESIGNING THE WALL

A dry-stone wall must be 'battered' – in other words, it must have a wide base and sides that slope inwards. For a wall about 1m (3ft 3in) in height (it is risky to build a dry-stone wall any higher) the base should be no less than 450mm (1ft 6in) wide. You should aim to provide a minimum slope of 25mm (1in) for every 600mm (2ft) of height.

Traditionally, the base of this type of wall rests on a 100mm (4in) bed of sand laid on compacted soil at the bottom of a shallow trench. For a more reliable foundation, lay a 100mm (4in) concrete footing, making it about 100mm (4in) wider than the wall on each side.

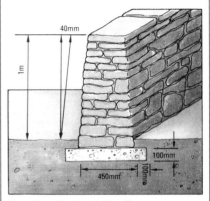

Proportions of a stone-built wall

Constructing the wall

Assuming you are using soil as a jointing material, spread a 25mm (1in) layer over the footing and place a substantial bonding stone across the width to form the bed of the first course (**1**). Lay other stones about the same height as the bonding stone along each side of the wall, pressing them down into the soil to make a firm base. It is worth stretching a builder's line along each side of the wall to help you make a reasonably straight base.

Lay smaller stones between to fill out the base of the wall (**2**), then pack more soil into all the crevices.

Spread another layer of soil on top of the base and lay a second course of stones, bridging the joints between the stones below (**3**). Press them down so that they angle inwards towards the centre of the wall. Check by eye that the coursing is about level as you build

the wall and remember to include bonding stones at regular intervals.

Introduce plants into the larger crevices or, alternatively, hammer smaller stones into the chinks to lock the large stones in place (**4**).

At the top of the wall, either fill the core with soil for plants or lay large, flat coping stones, firming them with packed soil. Finally, brush loose soil from the faces of the wall.

1 Lay a bonding stone at the end of the wall

2 Fill out the base with small stones

3 Lay a second course of stones

4 Fill the chinks

Retaining walls are designed to hold back a bank of earth, but don't attempt to cut into a steep bank and restrain it with a single high wall. Apart from the obvious dangers of the wall collapsing, terracing the slope with a series of low walls is a more attractive solution which offers opportunities for imaginative planting.

Choosing your materials

Bricks and concrete blocks are perfectly suitable materials to choose for constructing a retaining wall, provided it is sturdily built. It is best to support these walls with reinforcing bars buried in the concrete footing. Run the bars through hollow core blocks (**1**) or build a double skin of brickwork, rather like a miniature cavity wall, using wall ties to bind each skin together (**2**).

The mass and weight of natural stone make it ideal for retaining walls. The wall should be battered to an angle of 50mm (2in) to every 300mm (1ft) of height so that it virtually leans into the bank (**3**). Keep the height below 1m (3ft 3in) for safety. A skilful builder could construct a dry-stone retaining wall perfectly safely, but it pays to use mortar for additional rigidity.

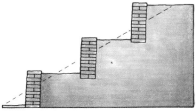
Terracing with retaining walls

1 A retaining wall of hollow concrete blocks

2 Use two skins of brick tied together

3 Lean a stone wall against the bank of earth

Constructing the wall

Excavate the soil to provide enough room to dig the footing and construct the wall. If the soil is loosely packed, restrain it temporarily with sheets of scrap plywood, corrugated iron or similar sheeting. Drive long metal pegs into the bank to hold the sheets in place (**1**). Lay the footing at the base of the bank and allow it to set before you begin building the wall.

Build a block or brick wall, using standard techniques. Lay uncut stones as if you were building a dry-stone wall, but set each course on mortar. If you use regular stone blocks, select stones of different proportions to add interest to the wall, and stagger the joints. Bed the stones in mortar.

It is essential to allow for drainage behind the wall to prevent the soil becoming waterlogged. When you lay the second course of stones embed 22mm (¾in) plastic pipes in the mortar bed, allowing them to slope slightly towards the front of the wall. The pipes should be placed at about 1m (3ft) intervals and pass right through the wall, projecting a little from the face (**2**).

1 Hold back the earth with scrap boards

2 Set plastic pipes in the wall for drainage

FINISHING STONE WALLS

When the wall is complete, rake out the joints to give a dry wall appearance. An old paintbrush is a useful tool for smoothing the mortar in deep crevices to make firm, watertight joints. Alternatively, point regular stones with concave rubbed joints.

Allow the mortar to set for a day or two before filling behind the wall. Lay hardcore at the base to cover the drainage pipes and pack shingle against the wall as you replace the soil. Provide a generous layer of topsoil so that you can plant up to the wall.

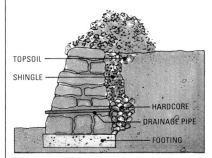

TOPSOIL
SHINGLE
HARDCORE
DRAINAGE PIPE
FOOTING

Filling behind a stone wall

PATHS, DRIVES AND PATIOS

For many people, paving of any kind is associated with the old 'back yard' environment, conjuring up an image of a concreted patch devoid of plants, trees and grass. In reality, introducing paving to a garden provides an opportunity to create contrasts of colour and texture which are intensified by sunlight and deep shade. A hard, unyielding surface is softened by the addition of foliage, while certain sculptural plants which recede into a background of soil and grass are seen to advantage against stone and gravel.

A paved patio
A paved area surrounded by stone or brick walls makes a perfect suntrap for swimming and relaxing.

Designing paved areas

The marriage of different materials offers numerous possibilities. It may be convenient to define areas of paving as paths, drives and patios, but they are only names to describe the function of those particular spaces in the garden. There is no reason why you cannot blend one area into another by using the same material throughout or employing similar colours to link one type of paving with another. On the other hand, you could take a completely different approach and deliberately juxtapose coarse and smooth textures or pale and dark tones to make one space stand out from the next.

Having so many choices at your disposal does have drawbacks; there is a strong temptation to experiment with any and every combination until the end result is a mishmash that is distracting to the eye. A few well-chosen materials which complement the house and its surroundings produce an effect which is much more appealing.

Working with concrete

Concrete might not be everybody's first choice for paving a garden, but it is a much more versatile material than is often realized. When cast into paving slabs, for example, it can be mistaken for natural stone, or it may be that the geometric pattern created by the combination of individual units attracts the eye while the material itself goes relatively unnoticed. Even ordinary concrete can be finished with a surprising variety of textures which dispel the drab image that concrete conjures up for many people.

THE INGREDIENTS OF CONCRETE

Concrete in its simplest form consists of cement and fine particles of stone – sand and pebbles – known as aggregate. The dry ingredients are mixed with water to create a chemical reaction with the cement which binds the aggregate into a hard, dense material. The initial hardening process takes place quite quickly. The mix becomes unworkable after a couple of hours depending on the temperature and humidity, but the concrete has no real strength for three to seven days. The hardening process continues for up to a month, or as long as there is moisture still present within the concrete. Moisture is essential to the reaction and consequently the concrete must not dry out too quickly during the first few days.

Cement

Standard Portland cement, sold in 50kg (110lb) bags from builders' merchants or DIY outlets, is used in the manufacture of concrete. In its dry condition it is a fine grey powder.

Sand

Sharp sand, a rather coarse and gritty material, constitutes part of the aggregate of a concrete mix. Don't buy fine builders' sand used for mortar, and avoid unwashed or beach sand, both of which contain impurities that could affect the quality of the concrete. Sharp sand is sold by the cubic metre (or cubic yard) from a builders' merchant, although it is perhaps more convenient to buy it in large plastic bags if you have to transport it by car or van.

Coarse aggregate

Coarse aggregate is gravel or crushed stone composed of particles large enough to be retained by a 5mm (¼in) sieve up to a maximum size of 20mm (¾in) for normal use. Once again, it can be bought loose by the cubic metre (cubic yard) or in smaller quantities packed in plastic sacks.

Pigments

Special pigments can be added to the concrete to colour it, but it is difficult to guarantee an even colour from one batch to another.

Combined aggregate

Naturally occurring sand-and-gravel mix, known as ballast, is sold as a combined aggregate for concreting. The proportion of sand to gravel is not guaranteed unless the ballast has been reconstituted to adjust the mix, and you may have to do it yourself. In any case, make sure it has been washed to remove impurities.

Dry-packed concrete

You can buy dry cement, sand and aggregate mixed to the required proportions for making concrete. Choose the proportion that best suits the job you have in mind. Concrete mix is sold in various size bags up to 50kg (110lb). Available from the usual outlets, it is a more expensive way of buying the ingredients, but is a simple and convenient method of ordering exactly the amount you will need. Before you add water to the mix, make sure the ingredients are mixed thoroughly.

Water

Use ordinary tap water to mix concrete, never river or sea water.

PVA admixture

You can buy a PVA admixture from builders' merchants to make a smoother concrete mix which is less susceptible to frost damage. Follow manufacturers' instructions for its use.

MIXING
CONCRETE

You can hire small mixing machines if you have to prepare a large volume of concrete, but for the average job it is just as convenient to mix it by hand. It isn't necessary to weigh the ingredients; simply mix them by volume, choosing the proportions that suit the job in hand.

Mixing by hand

Use large buckets to measure the ingredients, one for the cement and an identical one for the aggregate, in order to keep the cement perfectly dry. Different shovels are also a good idea. Measure the materials accurately, levelling them with the rim of the bucket. Tap the side of the bucket with the shovel as you load it with sand or cement so that the loose particles are shaken down.

Mix the sand and aggregate first on a hard, flat surface. Scoop a depression in the pile for the measure of cement, and mix all the ingredients until they form an even colour.

1 Mixing ingredients
Mix the ingredients by chopping the concrete mix with the shovel. Turn the mix over and chop again.

Form another depression and add some water from a watering can. Push the dry ingredients into the water from around the edge until surface water is absorbed, then mix the batch by chopping the concrete with the shovel (1). Add more water, turn the concrete from the bottom of the pile and chop it as before until the whole batch has an even consistency. To test the workability of the mix, form a series of ridges by dragging the back of the shovel across the pile (2). The surface of the concrete should be flat and even in texture, and the ridges should hold their shape without slumping.

2 Testing the mix
Make ridges with the back of the shovel to test the workability of the mix.

Mixing by machine

Make sure you set up the concrete mixer on a hard, level surface and that the drum is upright before you start the motor. Use a bucket to pour half the measure of coarse aggregate into the drum and add water. Add the sand and cement alternately in small batches, plus the rest of the aggregate. Keep on adding water little by little along with the other ingredients.

Let the batch mix for a few minutes, then tilt the drum of the mixer while it is still rotating and turn out a little concrete into a wheelbarrow so you can test its consistency (see above). If necessary, return the concrete to the mixer to adjust it.

Storing materials

If you buy sand and coarse aggregate in sacks, simply use as much as you need for the job in hand and keep the rest bagged up until required. If you buy them loose, store them in piles, divided by a wooden plank if necessary, on a hard surface or on thick polyethylene sheets. Protect them from rain with weighted sheets of plastic.

Storing cement is more critical. It is sold in paper sacks which will absorb moisture from the ground, so pile them on a board propped up on battens. Keep cement in a dry shed or garage if possible, and if you have to store it outdoors cover the bags with sheets of plastic weighted down with bricks. Once the bag is opened cement can absorb moisture from the air, so keep a partly used bag in a sealed plastic sack.

MACHINE SAFETY

- Make sure you understand the operating instructions before turning on the machine.
- Prop the mixer level and stable with blocks of wood.
- Never put your hands or shovel into the drum while the mixer is running.
- Don't lean over a rotating drum when you inspect the contents. It is good practice to wear goggles when mixing concrete.

READY-MIXED CONCRETE

If you need a lot of concrete for a driveway or large patio it may be worth ordering a delivery of ready-mixed concrete from a local supplier. Always contact the supplier well in advance to discuss your particular requirements. Specify the proportions of the ingredients and say whether you will require the addition of a retarding agent to slow down the setting time. (Once a normal mix of concrete is delivered, you will have no more than two hours in which to finish the job; a retarding agent can add up to two hours to the setting time.) Tell the supplier exactly what you need the concrete for and accept his advice. For quantities of less than 6cu m (8cu yd) you might have to shop around for a supplier who is willing to deliver without making an additional charge.

Talk over with the supplier any problems that may be involved in the delivery of the concrete. In order to avoid moving it too far by wheelbarrow, you will want it discharged as close to the site as possible, if not directly into place. However, the chute on a delivery truck can reach only so far, and if the vehicle is too large or heavy to drive onto your property you will need several helpers to move the concrete while it is still workable; a single cubic metre of concrete will fill 25 to 30 large wheelbarrows. If it takes longer than 30 to 40 minutes to discharge the load, you may have to pay extra.

Storing sand and aggregate
Separate the piles of sand and aggregate with a wooden plank.

Storing cement
Raise bags of cement off the ground and cover them with plastic sheeting.

● **Professional mixing**
There are companies who will deliver concrete ingredients and mix them to your specifications on the spot. All you have to do is barrow the concrete and pour it into place. There is no waste as you only pay for the concrete you use. Telephone a local company for details on price and minimum quantity.

41

DESIGNING CONCRETE PAVING

● **Sloping floors**
Although you can build upon a perfectly flat base, it is a good idea to slope the floor towards the door of a garage or outbuilding that is to be scrubbed out from time to time. Alternatively, slope a floor in two directions towards the middle to form a shallow drain that runs to the door.

The idea of having to design simple concrete pads and pathways might seem odd, but there are important factors to consider if the concrete is to be durable. At the least, you will have to decide on the thickness of the concrete that is needed to support the weight of traffic and the angle of slope required to drain off surface water. When the area of concrete is large or of a complicated shape, you must incorporate control joints to allow the material to expand and contract. If a pad is for a habitable building, it must include a damp-proof membrane to prevent moisture rising from the ground. Even the proportions of sand, cement and aggregate used in the mix must be considered carefully.

Deciding on the slope

A freestanding pad can be laid perfectly level, especially when it is supporting a small outbuilding, but a very slight slope or fall prevents water collecting in puddles if you have failed to get the concrete absolutely flat. When a pad is laid directly against a house it must have a definite fall away from the building, and any parking area or drive must shed water to provide adequate traction for vehicles and to minimize the formation of ice. When concrete is laid against a building, it must be at least 150mm (6in) below the existing damp-proof course.

USE OF PAVING	ANGLE OF FALL
Pathways	Not required
Drive	1 in 40 25mm per metre 1in per yard
Patio Parking space	1 in 60 away from building 16mm per metre ⅝in per yard
Pads for garages and outbuildings	1 in 80 towards the door 12.5mm per metre ½in per yard

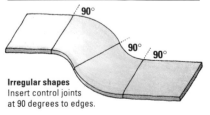

Irregular shapes
Insert control joints at 90 degrees to edges.

RECOMMENDED THICKNESSES FOR CONCRETE

The normal thicknesses recommended for concrete paving assume it will be laid on a firm subsoil, but if the soil is clay or peat, increase the thickness by about 50 per cent. The same applies to a new site where the soil might not be compacted. Unless the concrete is for pedestrian traffic only, lay a sub-base of compacted hardcore below the paving. This will absorb ground movement without affecting the concrete itself. A sub-base is not essential for a very lightweight structure like a small wooden shed, but as you might want to increase the weight at some time it is wise to install a sub-base at the outset.

Pathways

For pedestrian traffic only:
Concrete: 75mm (3in)
Sub-base: Not required

Light structures

A support pad for a wooden shed, coal bunker and so on:
Concrete: 75mm (3in)
Sub-base: 75mm (3in)

Patios

Any extensive area of concrete for pedestrian traffic:
Concrete: 100mm (4in)
Sub-base: 100mm (4in)

Parking spaces

Exposed paving for parking family car:
Concrete: 125mm (5in)
Sub-base: 150mm (6in)

Driveways

A drive which is used for an average family car only:
Concrete: 125mm (5in)
Sub-base: 150mm (6in)
For heavier vehicles like delivery trucks:
Concrete: 150mm (6in)
Sub-base: 150mm (6in)

Garages

Thicken up the edges of a garage pad to support the weight of the walls:
Concrete:
Floor: 125mm (5in)
Edges: 200mm (8in)
Sub-base:
Minimum 150mm (6in)

Allowing for expansion

Changes in temperature cause concrete to expand and contract. If this movement is allowed to happen at random, a pad or pathway will crack at the weakest or most vulnerable point. A control joint, composed of a compressible material, will absorb the movement or concentrate the force in predetermined areas where it does little harm. Joints should meet the sides of a concrete area at more or less 90 degrees. Always place a control joint between concrete and a wall, and around inspection chambers.

Positioning control joints
The exact position of control joints depends upon the area and shape of the concrete.

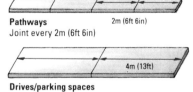

Pathways   2m (6ft 6in)
Joint every 2m (6ft 6in)

Drives/parking spaces
Joint every 4m (13ft)

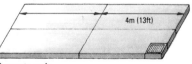

Concrete pads
Joints no more than 4m (13ft) apart and around inspection chambers.

Divide a pad into equal bays if:
● Length is more than twice the width.
● Longest dimension is more than 40 x thickness.
● Longest dimension exceeds 4m (13ft).

Estimate the amount of materials you require by calculating the volume of concrete in the finished pad, path or drive. Measure the surface area of the site and multiply that figure by the thickness of the concrete.

Estimating quantities of concrete

Use the gridded diagram to estimate the volume of concrete you will need by reading off the area of the site in square metres (square yards) and tracing it across horizontally to meet the angled line indicating the thickness of the concrete. Trace the line up to find the volume in cubic metres (cubic yards).

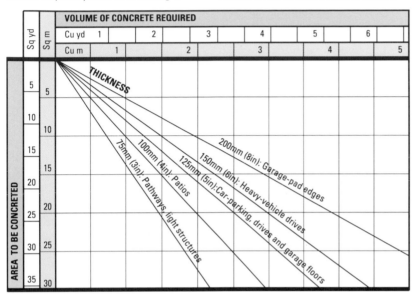

CALCULATING AREAS

Squares and rectangles
Calculate the area of rectangular paving by multiplying width by length:

Example:
2m x 3m = 6sq m
78in x 117in = 9126sq in or 7sq yd

Circles
Use the formula πr^2 to calculate the area of a circle. π = 3.14. r = radius of circle.

Example
3.14 x 2sq m = 3.14 x 4 = 12.56sq m
3.14 x 78sq in = 3.14 x 6084 = 19104sq in or 14.75sq yd

Irregular shapes
Draw an irregular area of paving on square paper. Count the whole squares and average out the portions to find the approximate area.

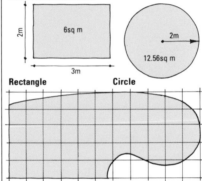

Rectangle   Circle

Square-up an irregular shape to calculate area

Estimating quantities of ingredients

Use the bar charts below to estimate the quantities of cement, sand and aggregate you will require to mix up the volume of concrete arrived at by using the chart above.

The figures are based on the quantity of ingredients required to mix one cubic metre of concrete for a particular type of mix, plus about 10 per cent in order to allow for wastage.

		1.00	1.50	2.00	2.50	3.00	3.50	4.00	4.50	5.00
GENERAL-PURPOSE MIX										
	Cement (50kg bags)	7.00	10.50	14.00	17.50	21.00	24.50	28.00	31.50	35.00
plus	Sand (cubic metres)	0.50	0.75	1.00	1.25	1.50	1.75	2.00	2.25	2.50
	Aggregate (cubic metres)	0.75	1.15	1.50	1.90	2.25	2.65	3.00	3.40	3.75
or	Ballast (cubic metres)	0.90	1.35	1.80	2.25	2.70	3.15	3.60	4.05	4.50
FOUNDATION MIX										
	Cement (50kg bags)	6.00	9.00	12.00	15.00	18.00	21.00	24.00	27.00	30.00
plus	Sand (cubic metres)	0.55	0.80	1.10	1.40	1.65	1.95	2.20	2.50	2.75
	Aggregate (cubic metres)	0.75	1.15	1.50	1.90	2.25	2.65	3.00	3.40	3.75
or	Ballast (cubic metres)	1.00	1.50	2.00	2.50	3.00	3.50	4.00	4.50	5.00
PAVING MIX										
	Cement (50kg bags)	9.00	13.50	18.00	22.50	27.00	31.50	36.00	40.50	45.00
plus	Sand (cubic metres)	0.45	0.70	0.90	1.15	1.35	1.60	1.80	2.00	2.25
	Aggregate (cubic metres)	0.75	1.15	1.50	1.90	2.25	2.65	3.00	3.40	3.75
or	Ballast (cubic metres)	1.00	1.50	2.00	2.50	3.00	3.50	4.00	4.50	5.00

CUBIC METRES OF CONCRETE

CLEANING TOOLS AND MACHINERY

Keep the shovel as clean as possible between mixing batches of concrete, and at the end of a working day wash all traces of concrete from your tools and wheelbarrow.

When you have finished using a concrete mixer, add a few shovels of coarse aggregate and a little water, then run the machine for a couple of minutes to scour the inside of the drum. Dump the aggregate, then hose out the drum with clean water.

Shovel unused concrete into sacks ready for disposal at a refuse dump and wash the mixing area with a stiff broom. Never hose concrete or any of the separate ingredients into a drain.

43

LAYING A CONCRETE PAD

Laying a simple pad as a base for a small shed or similar structure involves all the basic principles of concreting: building a retaining formwork, as well as the pouring, levelling and finishing of concrete. Provided the base is less than 2m (6ft 6in) square, there is no need to include control joints.

Mixing concrete by volume

Mixing the ingredients by volume is the easiest and most accurate way in which to guarantee the required proportions. Whatever container you use to measure the ingredients –shovel, bucket, wheelbarrow – the proportions remain the same.

MIXING CONCRETE BY VOLUME

Type of mix	Proportions		For 1cu m concrete
GENERAL PURPOSE			
Use in most situations including covered pads other than garage floors.	plus	1 part cement	6.4 bags (50kg)
		2 parts sand	0.448cu m
	or	3 parts aggregate	0.672cu m
		4 parts ballast	0.896cu m
FOUNDATION			
Use for footings at the base of masonry walls.	plus	1 part cement	5.6 bags (50kg)
		2½ parts sand	0.49cu m
	or	3½ parts aggregate	0.686cu m
		5 parts ballast	0.98cu m
PAVING			
Use for parking areas, drives, footpaths, and garage floors.	plus	1 part cement	8 bags (50kg)
		1½ parts sand	0.42cu m
	or	2½ parts aggregate	0.7cu m
		3½ parts ballast	0.98cu m

Excavating the site

Mark out the area of the pad with string lines attached to pegs driven into the ground outside the work area (1). Remove them to excavate the site, but replace them afterwards to help position the formwork which will hold the concrete in place.

Remove the topsoil and all vegetable matter within the site down to a level which allows for the combined thickness of concrete and sub-base. Extend the area of excavation about 150mm (6in) outside the space allowed for the pad. Cut back any roots you encounter and if there is any turf put it aside to cover the infill surrounding the completed pad. Level the bottom of the excavation by dragging a board across it (2), and compact the soil with a garden roller.

Erecting the formwork

Until the concrete sets hard it must be supported all round by formwork. For a straightforward rectangular pad, construct the formwork from 25mm (1in) thick softwood planks set on edge. The planks, which must be as wide as the finished depth of concrete, are held in place temporarily with stout 50 x 50mm (2 x 2in) wooden stakes. Second-hand or sawn timber is quite adequate. If it is slightly thinner than 25mm (1in), just use more stakes to brace it. If you have to join planks, butt them end to end, nailing a cleat on the outside (3).

Using the string lines as a guide, erect one board at the 'high' end of the pad, and drive stakes behind it at about 1m (3ft) intervals or less, with one for each corner. The tops of the stakes and board must be level and correspond exactly to the proposed surface of the pad. Nail the board to the stakes (4).

Set up another board opposite the first one, but before you nail it to the stakes, establish the crossfall with a spirit level and straightedge. Work out the difference in level from one end of the pad to the other. For example, a pad which is 2m (6ft 6in) long should drop 25mm (1in) over that distance. Tape a shim of timber to one end of the straightedge, and with the shim resting on the 'low' stakes, place the other end on the opposite board (5). Drive home each low stake until the spirit level reads horizontal, then nail the board flush with the tops of the stakes.

Erect the sides of the formwork, allowing the ends of the boards to overshoot the corners to make it easier to dismantle them when the concrete has set (6). Use the straightedge, this time without the shim, to level the boards across the formwork.

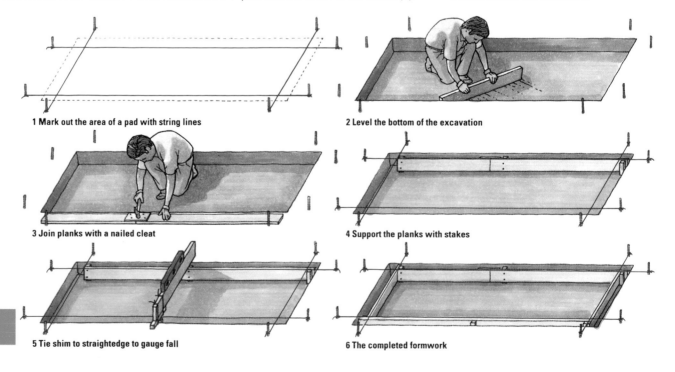

1 Mark out the area of a pad with string lines

2 Level the bottom of the excavation

3 Join planks with a nailed cleat

4 Support the planks with stakes

5 Tie shim to straightedge to gauge fall

6 The completed formwork

LAYING A CONCRETE PAD

SEE ALSO

Details for:	
Mixing concrete	41

Laying the sub-base

Hoggin, a mixture of gravel and sand, is an ideal material for a sub-base, but you can use crushed stone or brick provided you throw out any plaster, scrap metal or similar rubbish. Also remove large lumps of masonry as they will not compact well. Pour hardcore into the formwork and rake it fairly level before tamping it down with a heavy balk of timber (7). If there are any stubborn lumps, break them up with a heavy hammer. Fill in low spots with more hardcore or sharp sand until the sub-base comes up to the underside of the formwork boards.

Filling with concrete

Mix the concrete as near to the site as is practicable and transport the fresh mix to the formwork in a wheelbarrow. Set up firm runways of scaffold boards if the ground is soft, especially around the perimeter of the formwork. Dampen the sub-base and formwork with a fine spray and let surface water evaporate before tipping the concrete in place. Start filling from one end of the site and push the concrete firmly into the corners (8). Rake it level until the concrete stands about 18mm (¾in) above the level of the boards.

Tamp down the concrete with the edge of a 50mm (2in) thick plank that is long enough to reach across the formwork. Starting at one end of the site, compact the concrete with steady blows of the plank, moving it along by about half its thickness each time (9). Cover the whole area twice, then remove excess concrete, using the plank with a sawing action (10). Fill any low spots, then compact and level the concrete once more.

To retain the moisture, cover the pad with sheets of polyethylene, taped at the joints and weighted down with bricks around the edge (11). Alternatively, use wet sacking and keep it damp for three days by means of a fine spray. Try to avoid laying concrete in very cold weather, but if it is unavoidable, spread a layer of earth or sand on top of the sheeting to insulate the concrete from frost. You can walk on the concrete after three days, but leave it for about a week before removing the formwork and erecting a shed or similar outbuilding.

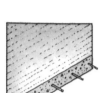

Extending a pad
If you want to enlarge a patio, simply butt a new section of concrete against the existing pad. The butt joint will form a control joint. To add a narrow strip, for a larger shed for example, drill holes in the edge of the pad and use epoxy adhesive to glue in short reinforcing rods before pouring the fresh concrete.

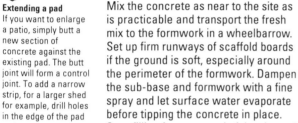

Finishing the edges
If any of the edges are exposed, the sharp corners might cause a painful injury. Radius the corners with a homemade edging float. Bend a piece of sheet metal over an 18mm (¾in) diameter rod or tube and screw a handle in the centre. Run the float along the formwork as you finish the surface of the concrete.

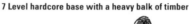

7 Level hardcore base with a heavy balk of timber

8 Pour the concrete, starting in the corners

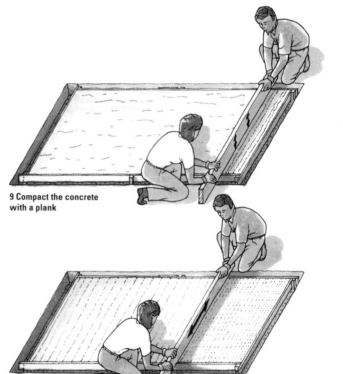

9 Compact the concrete with a plank

10 Use a sawing action to remove excess concrete

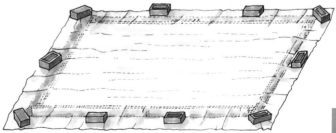

11 Cover the pad with weighted sheets of polyethylene

LAYING PATHS AND DRIVES

Paths and drives are laid and compacted in the same way as rectangular pads, using similar formwork to contain the concrete. However, the proportions of most paths and drives necessitate the inclusion of control joints to allow for expansion and contraction. You must install a sub-base beneath a drive, but a footpath can be laid on compacted soil levelled with sharp sand. Establish a slight fall across the site to shed rainwater. Don't use a vehicle on concrete for 10 days after laying.

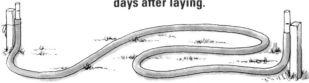

1 A water level made from a garden hose

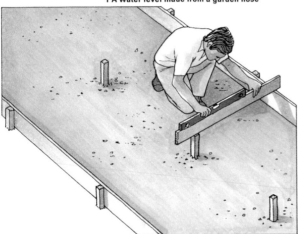

2 Level the formwork using a datum peg

DRAIN

A sloping drive
If you build a drive on a sloping site, make the transition from level ground as gentle as possible. If the drive runs towards a garage, let the last 2m (6ft) slope up towards the door. Use a pole to impress a drain across the wet concrete at the lowest point.

5 Support board with concrete and nails

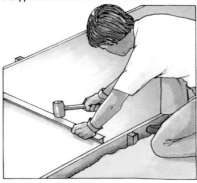

6 Make a dummy joint with T-section metal

Setting out paths and drives

Excavate the site, allowing for the thickness of sub-base and concrete. Level the bottom of the excavation as accurately as you can, using a board to scrape the surface flat.

Drive accurately levelled pegs into the ground along the site to act as datum points for the formwork. Space them about 2m (6ft 6in) apart down the centre of the pathway. Drive in the first peg until its top corresponds exactly to the proposed surface of the concrete. Use a long straightedge and spirit level or, better still, a home-made water level to position every other peg. To make the latter, push a short length of transparent plastic tubing into each end of an ordinary garden hose. Fill the hose with water until it appears in the tube at both ends. As long as the ends remain open, the water level at each end is constant so that you can establish a level over any distance, even around obstacles or corners. Tie one end of the hose to the first datum peg so that the water level aligns with the top of the peg. Use the other to establish the level of every other peg along the pathway (1). Cork each end of the hose to retain the water as you move it.

To set a fall with a water level, make a mark on one tube below the surface of the water and use that as a gauge for the top of the peg.

Erecting formwork

Construct formwork from 25mm (1in) thick planks as for a concrete pad. To check it is level, rest a straightedge on the nearest datum peg (2).

If the drive or path is very long, timber formwork can be expensive. It might be cheaper to hire metal 'road forms' (3). Straight-sided formwork is made from rigid units, but flexible sections are available to form curves.

If you want to bend wooden formwork, make a series of parallel saw cuts across the width of the plank in the area of the curve (4). The timber is less likely to snap if you place the saw cuts on the inside of the bend.

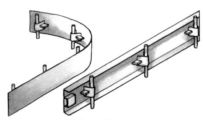

3 Curved and straight road forms

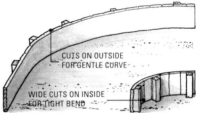

CUTS ON OUTSIDE FOR GENTLE CURVE

WIDE CUTS ON INSIDE FOR TIGHT BEND

4 Curved formwork made with wooden planks

Installing control joints

Install a permanent expansion joint every 2m (6ft 6in) for a footpath and every 4m (13ft) along a drive. Cut strips of rot-proofed hardboard or 12mm (½in) thick softwood to fit exactly between the formwork and to match the depth of the concrete. Before pouring, hold the control joints in place with mounds of concrete and nails on each side of the board driven into the formwork (5). Pack more concrete carefully on each side of the joints as you fill the formwork and tamp towards them from both sides so that they are not dislodged.

As the joints are permanent fixtures, make sure they are level with the surface of the concrete. Install similar joints in a patio or use an alternate-bay construction (see opposite page).

To prevent concrete cracking between joints on a narrow path, cut 18mm (¾in) deep grooves across the compacted concrete to form dummy joints alternating with the physical ones. The simplest method is to cut a length of T-section metal to fit between the formwork boards. Place it on the surface of the wet concrete and tap it down with a mallet (6). Carefully lift the strip out of the concrete to leave a neat impression. If the concrete should move, a crack will develop unnoticed at the bottom of the groove.

Place strips of thick bituminous felt between concrete and an adjoining wall to absorb expansion. Hold the felt in place with mounds of concrete, as described left, before pouring the full amount of concrete.

CONCRETE
LAYING

SURFACE
FINISHES FOR
CONCRETE

SEE ALSO

Details for:	
Control joints	42
Tamping concrete	45
Preservers	70

ALTERNATE-BAY METHOD OF CONSTRUCTION

It is not always possible to lay all the concrete in one operation. In such cases it is easier to divide the formwork crosswise with additional planks known as stop ends to form equal-size bays. By filling alternate bays with concrete, you have plenty of time to compact and level each section and more room in which to manoeuvre. It is a convenient way to lay a large patio which would be practically impossible to compact and level in one go, and it is the only method to use for drives or paths butting against a wall which makes it impossible to work across the width. Alternate-bay construction is often used for drives on a steep slope to prevent heavy, wet concrete from slumping downhill.

There is no need to install control joints when using bay construction, but you may want to form dummy joints for a neat appearance (see opposite).

Concreting alternate bays
Stand in the empty bays to compact concrete laid against a wall. When the first bays are set hard, remove the stop ends and fill the gaps, using the surface of the firm concrete as a level.

INSPECTION CHAMBERS

Prevent expansion damaging an inspection chamber by surrounding it with control joints. Place formwork around the chamber and fill with concrete. When set, remove the boards and place felt strips or preserver-treated softwood boards on all sides.

Surround an inspection chamber with formwork

The surface finishes produced by tamping or striking off with a sawing action are perfectly adequate for a skid-proof, workmanlike surface for a pad, drive or pathway, but you can produce a range of other finishes using simple handtools once you have compacted and levelled the concrete.

Float finishes
Smooth the tamped concrete by sweeping a wooden float across the surface, or make an even finer texture by finishing with a trowel (steel float). Let the concrete dry out a little before using a float or you will bring water to the top and weaken it, which will eventually result in a dusty residue on the hardened concrete. Bridge the formwork with a stout plank so that you can reach the centre, or hire a skip float with a long handle for large pads.

Make a smooth finish with a wooden float

Brush finishes
Make a finely textured surface by drawing a yard broom across the setting concrete. Flatten the concrete initially with a wooden float, then make parallel passes with the broom held at a low angle to avoid 'tearing' the surface.

Texture the surface with a broom

Brush-finishing concrete

Exposed-aggregate finish
Embedding small stones or pebbles in the surface makes a very attractive and practical finish, but you will need a little practice in order to do it successfully.

Scatter dampened pebbles onto the freshly laid concrete and tamp them firmly with a length of timber until they are flush with the surface (**1**). Place a plank across the formwork and apply your full weight to make sure the surface is even. Leave to harden for a while until all surface water has evaporated, then use a very fine spray and a brush to wash away the cement from around the pebbles until they protrude (**2**). Cover the concrete for about 24 hours, then lightly wash the surface again to clean any sediment off the pebbles. Cover the concrete again and leave it to harden thoroughly.

1 Tamp pebbles into fresh concrete

2 Wash the cement from around the pebbles

Exposed-aggregate finish

PAVING SLABS

SEE ALSO
Details for:
Brick pavers   51

If your only experience of paving slabs is the rather bland variety used for public footpaths, then cast-concrete paving may not seem a very attractive proposition for a garden. However, manufacturers can supply more pleasing products in a wide range of shapes, colours and finishes.

Colours and textures

Paving slabs are made by hydraulic pressing or casting in moulds to create the desired surface finish. Pigments and selected aggregates added to the concrete mix create the illusion of natural stone or a range of muted colours. Combining two or more colours within the same area of paving can be very striking.

1 Cobbles or sets
Large slabs resemble an area of smaller cobbles or sets. Careful laying and filling are essential for success. Sets are 'laid' either in straight rows or as curves.

2 Planter
Four planter stones laid in a square leave a circle in which to plant a tree or shrub.

3 Exposed aggregate
Crushed-stone aggregate has a very pleasing mottled appearance, either exposed to make a coarse gritstone texture or polished flat to resemble terrazzo.

4 Brushed finishes
A brush-finished slab, textured with parallel grooves as if a stiff broom had been dragged across the wet concrete, has a practical non-slip surface. Straight or swirling patterns are available.

5 Riven stone
The finish resembles that of natural stone. The best-quality slabs are cast from real-stone originals in a wide variety of subtle textures. If the texture continues over the edge of the slabs, they can be used for steps and coping.

SHAPES AND SIZES

Although some manufacturers offer a wider choice than others, there is a fairly standard range of shapes and modular sizes. You can carry the largest slabs single-handed, but it is a good idea to have an assistant when manoeuvring them carefully into place.

Square and rectangular
A single size and shape makes grid-like patterns or, when staggered, creates a bonded brickwork effect. Rectangular slabs can form a basket-weave or herringbone pattern. Alternatively, combine different sizes so as to create the impression of random paving.

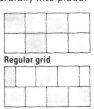
Regular grid

Staggered slabs

Basket-weave pattern

Herringbone pattern

Random paving

Hexagonal
Hexagonal slabs form honeycomb patterns. Use half slabs, running across flats or from point to point, to edge areas that are paved in straight lines.

Half-hexagonal slabs

Hexagonal slab

Honeycomb pattern

Tapered slabs
Use tapered slabs as edging for ponds, around trees, and for curved paths or steps. Lay them head to toe to make straight sections of paving. Use right-handed or left-handed half slabs at the ends.

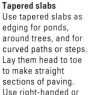
Full and half-tapered slabs

Straight section

Circular
Circular slabs make perfect individual stepping stones across a lawn or flower bed, but for a wide area fill the spaces between with cobbles or gravel.

Butted circular slabs

Laying heavy paving slabs involves a good deal of physical labour, but in terms of technique it is no more complicated than tiling a wall. Accurate setting out and careful laying, especially during the early stages, will produce perfect results. Take extra care when you lay hexagonal slabs to ensure that the last few slabs fit properly.

CUTTING CONCRETE SLABS

Mark a line across a slab with a soft pencil or chalk. Using a bolster and hammer, chisel a groove about 3mm (⅛in) deep along the line (1). Continue the groove down both edges and across the underside of the slab. Place the slab on a bed of sand and put a block of wood at one end of the groove. Strike the block with a hammer while moving it along the groove until the slab splits (2). Clean up the edge with a bolster.

For a perfect cut, hire an angle grinder fitted with a stone-cutting disc. Using the grinder, score a deep groove as before. Tap along the groove with a bolster until the slab splits.

1 Cut a groove with a bolster chisel

2 Strike block over groove with a hammer

PROTECTING YOUR EYES

When cutting slabs with a chisel or an angle grinder, always protect your eyes with plastic goggles. An angle grinder throws up a great deal of dust, so wear a simple gauze facemask too as a safeguard.

Setting out the area of paving

Wherever possible, to eliminate the arduous task of cutting units to fit, plan an area of paving to be laid with whole slabs only. Use a straight wall as a datum line and measure away from it, or allow for a 100 to 150mm (4 to 6in) margin of gravel between the paving and wall if the location dictates that you have to lay slabs towards the house. A gravel margin not only saves time and money by using fewer slabs, but also provides an area for planting climbers and for adequate drainage to keep the wall dry. Even so, establish a 16mm per metre (⅝ in per yard) slope across the

paving so that most surface water will drain into the garden. Any paving must be 150mm (6in) below a damp-proof course to protect the building.

As paving slabs are made to fairly precise dimensions, marking out an area simply involves accurate measurement, allowing for a 6 to 8mm (¼in) gap between slabs. Some slabs are cast with sloping edges to provide a tapered joint (1) and should be butted edge to edge. Employ pegs and string to mark out the perimeter of the paved area, and check your measurements before you excavate.

1 Tapered joint

Preparing a base for paving

Paving slabs must be laid upon a firm, level base, but the depth and substance of that base depends on the type of soil and the proposed use of the paving.

For straightforward patios and paths, remove vegetable matter and topsoil to allow for the thickness of the slabs, a 25mm (1in) layer of sharp sand and an extra 18mm (¾in) so that the paving will be below the level of surrounding turf and thus will not damage your lawn mower. Compact the soil with a garden

roller, spread the sand with a rake and level it by scraping and tamping with a length of timber (2).

To support heavier loads, or if the soil is composed of clay or peat, lay a sub-base of firmly compacted hardcore – broken bricks or crushed stone – to a depth of 75 to 100mm (3 to 4in) before spreading the sand to level the surface.

If you plan to park vehicles on the paving, increase the depth of hardcore to 150mm (6in).

2 Level the sand base

Laying the paving slabs

Set up string lines again as a guide and lay the edging slabs on the sand, working in both directions from a corner. When you are satisfied with their positions, lift them one at a time and set them on a bed of mortar (1 part cement : 4 parts sand). Add just enough water to make a firm mortar. Lay a fist-size blob under each corner and one more to support the centre of the slab (3). If you intend to drive vehicles across the slabs, lay a continuous bed of mortar about 50mm (2in) thick.

Lay three slabs at a time with 6mm (¼in) wooden spacers between. Level each slab by tapping with a heavy hammer, using a block of wood (4). Check the alignment.

Gauge the slope across the paving by setting up datum pegs along the high side. Drive them into the ground until the top of each corresponds to the finished surface of the paving, then use the straightedge to check the fall on the slabs (5). Lay the remainder of the slabs, working out from the corner each time to keep the joints square. Remove the spacers before the mortar sets.

3 Lay blobs of mortar

4 Level the slabs

5 Check the fall with a spirit level

Filling the joints

Don't walk on the paving for two to three days until the mortar has set. If you have to cross the area, lay planks across the slabs to spread the load.

To fill the gaps between the slabs, brush a dry mortar mix of 1 part cement : 3 parts sand into the open joints (6). Remove any surplus material from the surface of the paving, then sprinkle the area with a very fine spray of water to consolidate the mortar. Avoid dry mortaring if heavy rain is imminent; it may wash the mortar out.

6 Fill the joints

LAYING
CRAZY PAVING

The informal nature of paths or patios laid with irregular-shaped paving stones has always been popular. The random effect, which many people find more appealing than the geometric accuracy of neatly laid slabs, is also very easy to achieve. A good eye for shape and proportion is more important than a practised technique.

Materials for crazing paving

You can use broken concrete slabs if you can find enough but, in terms of appearance, nothing compares with natural riven stone. Stratified rock which splits into thin layers of its own accord as it is quarried is ideal for crazy paving, and can be obtained at a very reasonable price if you can collect it yourself. Select stones which are approximately 40 to 50mm (1½ to 2in) thick in a variety of shapes and sizes.

Crazy paving made with broken concrete slabs

SETTING OUT AND LAYING A BASE

You can set out string lines to define straight edges to crazy paving, although they will never be as precisely defined as those formed with regular cast-concrete slabs. Alternatively, allow the stones to form an irregular junction with grass or shingle, perhaps setting one or two stones out from the edge.

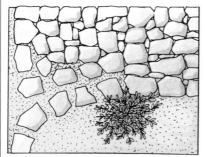
Create an irregular edge to crazy paving

Arrange an area of stones, selecting them for a close fit but avoiding too many straight, continuous joints. Trim those that don't quite fit with a bolster and hammer. Reserve larger stones for the perimeter of the paved area as small stones tend to break away.

Use a mallet or block of wood and a hammer to bed each stone into the sand (1) until they are all perfectly stable and reasonably level. Having bedded an area of about 1sq m (1sq yd), use a straightedge and spirit level to true up the stones (2). If necessary, add

or remove sand beneath individual stones until the area is level. When the main area is complete, fill in the larger gaps with small stones, tapping them into place with a mallet (3).

Fill the joints by spreading more sand across the paving and sweeping it into the joints from all directions (4). Alternatively, mix up a stiff, almost dry, mortar and press it into the joints with a trowel, leaving no gaps.

Use an old paintbrush to smooth the mortared joints and wipe the stones clean with a damp sponge.

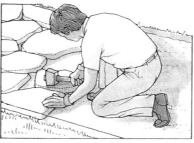
1 Bed the stones in the sand base

2 Check the level across several stones

3 Fill the gaps with small stones

4 Sweep dry sand into the joints

Place individual stones or slabs across a lawn to form a row of stepping stones. Cut around the edge of each stone with a spade or trowel and remove the area of turf directly beneath. Scoop out the earth to allow for a 25mm (1in) bed of sharp sand plus the stone, which must be about 18mm (¾in) below the level of the surrounding turf. Tap the stone into the sand until it no longer rocks when you step on it.

Cut around a stepping stone with a trowel

Stepping stones preserve a lawn

PAVING WITH BRICK SYSTEMS

BRICK PATTERNS

Concrete bricks have one surface face with chamfered edges all round, and spacers moulded into the sides to form accurate joints. Housebricks can be laid on edge or face down showing the wide face normally unseen in a wall.

Unlike brick walls, which must be bonded in a certain way for stability, brick paths can be laid to any pattern that appeals to you.

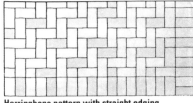
Herringbone pattern with straight edging

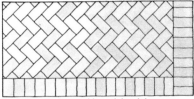
Angled herringbone with straight edging

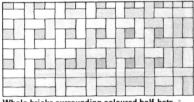
Whole bricks surrounding coloured half-bats

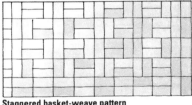
Staggered basket-weave pattern

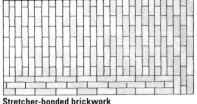
Stretcher-bonded brickwork

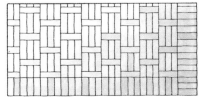
Cane-weave pattern

Bricks make charming paths. The wide variety of textures and colours available offers endless possibilities of pattern, but do choose the type of brick carefully, bearing in mind the sort of use your paving can expect.

Materials for brick paving

Ordinary housebricks are often used for paths and small patios, even though there is the risk of spalling in freezing conditions unless they happen to be engineering bricks. The slightly uneven texture and colour are the very reasons why second-hand bricks are so much in demand for garden paving, so a little frost damage is usually acceptable.

Housebricks are not really suitable if the paved area is to be a parking space or drive, especially if it is to be used by heavy vehicles. For a durable surface, even under severe conditions, use concrete bricks instead. These are slightly smaller than standard housebricks, being 200 x 100 x 65mm (8 x 4 x 2½in). Red or grey are widely available and you can obtain other colours by special order.

Brick pavers
Clay brick pavers *(top row)* are made in a wide variety of colours and textures. Concrete pavers *(bottom row)* are less colourful but more shapes are available.

Providing a base for brick paving

Lay brick footpaths and patios on a 75mm (3in) hardcore base covered with a 50mm (2in) layer of sharp sand. If you are laying concrete bricks for a drive, increase the depth of hardcore to 150mm (6in).

Fully compact the hardcore and fill all voids so that sand from the bedding course is not lost to the sub-base.

Provide a cross-fall on patios and drives as for concrete, and make sure that the surface of the paving is at least 150mm (6in) below a damp-proof course to protect the building.

Retaining edges

Unless the brick path is laid against a wall or some similar structure, the edges of the paving must be contained by a permanent restraint. Timber, treated with a chemical preserver, is one solution, constructed like the formwork for concrete. The edging boards should be flush with the surface of the path, but drive the stakes below ground so that they can be covered by soil or turf (1).

As an alternative, set an edging of bricks in concrete. Dig a trench deep and wide enough to accommodate a row of bricks on end plus a 100mm (4in) concrete 'foundation'. Lay the bricks while the concrete is still wet, holding them in place temporarily with a staked board while you pack more concrete behind the edging. When the concrete has set, remove the board and lay hardcore and sand in the excavation.

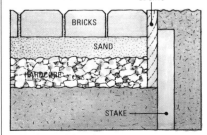
1 Wooden retaining edge

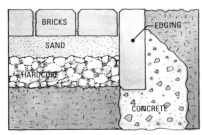
2 Brick retaining edge

51

LAYING THE BRICKS

Having chosen your bricks, prepared the ground and set retaining edges you can start laying your paving. When bricks are first laid upon the sand they should project 10mm (⅜in) above the edging restraints to allow for bedding them in at a later stage (**1**). To level the sand for a path, cut a notched spreader to span the edging (**2**). If the paving is too wide for a spreader, lay levelling battens on the hardcore base and scrape the sand to the required depth using a straightedge (**3**). Remove the battens and fill the voids carefully with sand. Keep the sand bed dry at all times. If it rains before you can lay the bricks, either let the sand dry out thoroughly or replace it with dry sand.

Lay an area of bricks on the sand to your chosen pattern. Work from one end of the site, kneeling on a board placed across the bricks (**4**). Never stand on the bed of sand. Lay whole bricks only, leaving any gaps at the edges to be filled with cut bricks after you have laid an area of approximately 1 to 2sq m (1 to 2½sq yd). Concrete bricks have fixed spacers, so butt them together tightly.

Fill any remaining spaces with bricks cut with a bolster. If you are paving a large area you can hire an hydraulic guillotine (see left).

When the area of paving is complete, tamp the bricks into the sand bed by striking a stout batten with a heavy club hammer. The batten must be large enough to cover several bricks to maintain the level (**5**). For a professional finish, hire a powerful plate vibrator(**6**). Pass the vibrator over the paved area two or three times until it has worked the bricks down into the sand and flush with the outer edging. Vibrating the bricks will work some sand up between them; complete the job by brushing more sand across the finished paving and vibrating it into the open joints.

Cutting bricks
Hire an hydraulic brick-cutting guillotine to cut pavers.

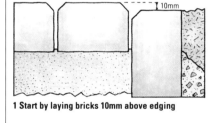

1 Start by laying bricks 10mm above edging

2 Level the sand with a notched spreader

3 Or lay levelling battens on the hardcore

4 Lay the bricks to your chosen pattern

5 Tamp the bricks with a hammer and batten

6 A vibrator levels brick paving perfectly

Plain concrete-brick drive and parking space

Mottled-brick garden path

Interlocking concrete pavers

Bricks laid to a herringbone pattern

COBBLESTONES AND GRAVEL

Cobblestones and gravel are used more for their decorative quality than for functional paving for drives or pathways. Cobbles in particular are most uncomfortable to walk on and, although a firmly consolidated area of gravel is fine for vehicles, walking on a gravel footpath can be rather heavy going. Both materials come into their own, however, when used as a foil for areas of flat paving slabs or bricks, and to set off plants such as dwarf conifers and heathers.

Laying cobbles

Cobbles – large flint pebbles found on many a beach – can be laid loose, perhaps with larger rocks and plants. However, they are often set in mortar or concrete to create more formal areas.

Consolidate a layer of hardcore and cover it with a levelled layer of dry concrete mix about 50mm (2in) deep.

Press the cobbles into the dry mix, packing them tightly together and leaving them projecting well above the surface. Use a stout batten to tamp the area level (1), then lightly sprinkle the whole area with water, both to set off the concrete-hardening process and to clean the surfaces of the cobbles.

Large cobbles as a background to plants

1 Tamp the cobbles into a dry concrete mix

Laying gravel

If an area of gravel is to be used as a pathway or for motor vehicles, construct retaining edges of brick, concrete kerbs or wooden boards as for brick paths. This will stop gravel being spread outside its allotted area.

To construct a gravel drive, the sub-base and the gravel itself must be compacted and levelled to prevent cars skidding and churning up the material. Lay a 150mm (6in) bed of firmed hardcore topped with 50mm (2in) of very coarse gravel mixed with sand. Roll it flat. Rake an 18 to 25mm (¾ to 1in) layer of fine 'pea' gravel across the sub-base and roll it down to make it firm.

Making a gravel garden
To lay an area of gravel for planting, simply excavate the soil to accept a 25mm (1in) deep bed of fine gravel. Either set the gravel 18mm (¾in) below the level of the lawn or edge the gravel garden with bricks or flat stones. Scrape away a small area of gravel to allow for planting, then sprinkle the gravel back again to cover the soil right up to the plant.

Gravel-and-conifer garden ▶

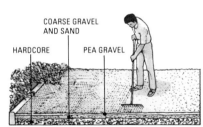
COARSE GRAVEL AND SAND
HARDCORE   PEA GRAVEL
Rake pea gravel across the surface of a drive

WOODEN PATHWAYS

If you live in a rural district where large logs are plentiful or perhaps a mature tree has been felled in your garden, you can use 150mm (6in) lengths of sawn timber set on end to make a practical and charming footpath. Lay the logs together like crazy paving or use large pieces of wood as stepping stones. Hold wood rot at bay by soaking the sawn sections in chemical preserver.

Laying a log pathway
Excavate the area of the pathway to a depth of 200mm (8in) and spread a 50mm (2in) deep layer of gravel and sand mix across the bottom. Use concreting ballast – combined aggregate – or make up the mix yourself. Level the bed by scraping and tamping with a straightedge.

Place the logs on end on the bed, arranging them to create a pleasing combination of shapes and sizes (1). Work them into the sand until they stand firmly and evenly, then pour more sand and gravel between them (2). Brush the material across the pathway in all directions until the gaps between the logs are filled flush with the surface (3). If any logs stand proud so that they could cause someone to trip, tap them down with a heavy hammer.

If you want to plant between the logs, scrape out some sand and gravel and replace it with the appropriate soil.

1 Arrange the logs on end

2 Shovel sand-and-gravel mix between the logs

3 Brush more mix into the joints

● **Use a heavy roller**
A lightweight garden roller is fine for compacting earth or sand, but use one weighing about 100kg (2cwt) when levelling hardcore.

RESURFACING WITH TARMAC

● **Laying a new path**
Although cold-cure tarmac is primarily a resurfacing material, it can be applied to a new hardcore base that has been compacted firmly, levelled and sealed with a slightly more generous coat of bitumen emulsion.

● **Treating for heavy wear**
At entrances to drives and on bends, vehicle tyres cause more wear than normal. Treat these areas with an 18mm (¾in) rolled layer of cold-cure tarmac (see far right) before applying a dressing of stone chippings.

● **Double dressing**
If the surface you are dressing is in a very poor condition or exceptionally loose, apply a first coat of bitumen emulsion. Cover with chippings and roll thoroughly. Two days later sweep away loose chippings and apply a second coat of emulsion and finish with chippings as described right.

DRESSING WITH STONE CHIPPINGS

As an alternative to tarmac, completely resurface a path or drive with natural-stone chippings embedded in fresh bitumen emulsion. Chippings in various colours are available in 25kg (55lb) sacks which cover about 2.5sq m (3sq yd). Apply weedkiller and fill potholes as for tarmac (see right).

Bitumen emulsion sets by evaporation in about 12 hours, but until that time it is not completely waterproof so check the weather forecast to avoid wet conditions. You can lay emulsion on a damp surface, but not on an icy one.

Apply emulsion, available in 5, 25 and 200kg (11, 55 and 440lb) drums. A 5kg drum will cover about 7sq m (8sq yd), provided the surface is dense macadam or concrete. However, an open-textured surface will absorb considerably more bitumen emulsion.

Decant the emulsion into a bucket to make it easier to pour onto the surface, and brush it out, not too thinly, with a stiff broom as for laying tarmac (see right). Having brushed out one bucket of emulsion, spread the stone chippings evenly with a spade. Hold the spade horizontally just above the surface and gently shake the chippings off the edge of the blade **(1)**. Don't pile them too thickly, but make sure the emulsion is covered completely. Cover an area of about 5sq m (6sq yd), then roll the chippings down. When the entire area is covered, roll it once more. If traces of bitumen show between the chippings, mask them with a little sharp sand and roll again. (See margin notes left for applying dressing to heavy-wear areas.)

You can walk or drive on the dressed surface immediately. One week later, gently sweep away surplus chippings. Patch any bare areas by re-treating them with emulsion and chippings.

1 Sprinkle a layer of chippings with a spade

Smarten up an old tarmac path or drive, or any sound but unsightly paved area, by resurfacing with cold-cure tarmac. It makes a serviceable surface and is ready to lay from the sack. Roll it flat with a garden roller; a light one will do, although you will have to make extra passes.

Choosing the materials

Choose between red or black tarmac. It is available in 25kg (55lb) sacks, which will cover about 0.9sq m (10sq ft) at a thickness of 12mm (½in). Each sack contains a separate bag of decorative stone chippings for embedding in the soft tarmac as an alternative finish. Cold-cure tarmac can be laid in any weather, but it is much easier to level and roll flat on a warm, dry day. If you have to work in cold weather, store the materials in a warm place the night before laying. While it is not essential, edging the tarmac with bricks, concrete kerbs or wooden boards will improve the appearance of the finished surface.

Preparing the surface

Pull up all weeds and grass growing between the old paving, then apply a strong weedkiller to the surface two days before you lay the tarmac. Sweep the area clean, and level any potholes; cut the sides vertical, remove dust and debris from the hole, then paint with bitumen emulsion supplied by the tarmac manufacturer. Wait for it to turn black before filling the hole with 18mm (¾in) layers of tarmac, compacting each layer until the surface is level.

Apply a tack coat of bitumen emulsion to the entire surface to make a firm bond between the new tarmac and the old paving. Mask surrounding walls, kerb stones and manhole covers. Stir the emulsion with a stick before pouring it from its container, then spread it thinly with a stiff-bristled broom. Try not to splash, and avoid leaving puddles, especially at the foot of a slope. Leave the tack coat to set for about 20 minutes and, in the meantime, wash the broom in hot, soapy water. Don't apply the tack coat when it is likely to rain.

Apply a tack coat of bitumen emulsion

Applying the tarmac

Rake the tarmac to make a layer about 18mm (¾in) thick **(1)**, using a straightedge to scrape the surface flat. Press down any stubborn lumps with your foot. Spread the contents of no more than three sacks before the initial rolling. Keep the roller wet **(2)** to avoid picking up specks of tarmac. Don't run the roller onto grass or gravel or you may roll particles into the tarmac.

Spread and roll tarmac over the whole area, then achieve the final compaction by rolling it thoroughly in several directions. Lightly scatter the chippings **(3)** prior to the final pass.

You can walk on the tarmac immediately, but avoid wearing high-heeled shoes. Don't drive on it for a day or two, and if you have to erect a ladder on it spread the load by placing a board under the ladder. You should always protect tarmac from oil and petrol spillage, but take special care while the surface is fresh.

1 Level the tarmac

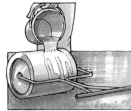
2 Keep the roller wet

3 Scatter chippings

BUILDING
GARDEN STEPS

Designing a garden for a sloping site offers many possibilities for creating attractive changes of level by terracing areas of paving or holding planting beds in place with retaining walls. However, moving safely from one level to another requires at least one flight of steps.

Designing steps

If you are fortunate enough to own a large garden, and the slope is very gradual, a series of steps with wide treads and low risers can make an impressive feature. If the slope is steep, you can avoid a 'staircase' appearance by constructing a flight of steps composed of a few treads interposed with wide, flat landings, at which points the flight can change direction to add further interest and offer a different viewpoint of the garden. In fact, a shallow flight can be virtually a series of landings, perhaps circular in plan, sweeping up the slope in a curve.

For the steps to be both comfortable and safe to use, the proportion of tread (the part you stand on) to riser (the vertical part of the step) is important. As a rough guide, construct steps so that the depth of the tread (from front to back) plus twice the height of the riser equals 650mm (2ft 2in). For example, match 300mm (1ft) treads with 175mm (7in) risers, 350mm (1ft 2in) treads with 150mm (6in) risers and so on. Never make treads less than 300mm (1ft) deep or risers higher than 175mm (7in).

Garden steps built with natural stone

Concrete paving slabs in their various forms are ideal for making firm, flat treads for garden steps. Construct the risers from concrete facing blocks or bricks, allowing the treads to overhang by 25 to 50mm (1 to 2in) to cast an attractive shadow line which also defines the edge of the step.

Measure the difference in height from the top of the slope to the bottom to gauge the number of steps required. Mark the position of the risers with pegs and roughly shape the steps in the soil as a confirmation (**1**).

Either lay concrete slabs, bedded in sand, flush with the ground at the foot of the slope or dig a trench for hardcore and a 100 to 150mm (4 to 6in) concrete base to support the first riser (**2**). When the concrete has set, construct the riser using normal bricklaying methods and check its alignment with a spirit level (**3**). Fill behind the riser with compacted hardcore until it is level, then lay the tread on a bed of mortar (**4**). Using a spirit level as a guide, tap down the tread until it slopes very slightly towards its front edge to shed rainwater and so prevent ice forming in cold weather.

Measure from the front edge of the tread to mark the position of the next riser on the slabs (**5**), and construct the step in the same way. Set the final tread flush with the area of paving, pathway or lawn at the top of the flight of steps.

Dealing with the sides

It is usually possible to landscape the slope at each side of the flight of steps, and turf or plant it to prevent the soil washing down onto the steps.

Alternatively, extend the riser to edge each tread or build a wall or planter on each side of the steps. Another solution is to retain the soil with large stones, perhaps extending into a rockery on one or both sides.

1 Cut the shape of the steps in the soil

2 Dig the footing for the first riser

3 Build a brick riser and level it

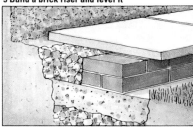

4 Lay the tread on mortar

5 Mark the position of the next riser

Concrete-slab steps
A section through a simple flight of garden steps built with brick risers and concrete-slab treads.
1 Concrete footing
2 Brick-built riser
3 Hardcore infill
4 Concrete-slab tread

CURVED STEPS/
LOG STEPS

● **Dealing with slippery steps**
Algae will grow in damp conditions, especially under trees, and steps can become dangerously slippery if it is allowed to build up on the surfaces. Brush with a solution of 1 part household bleach : 4 parts water. After 48 hours, wash with clean water and repeat if the fungal growth is heavy. You can also use a proprietary fungicidal solution, but follow manufacturers' instructions carefully.

BUILDING GARDEN STEPS

Casting new steps in concrete needs such complicated formwork that the end result hardly justifies the amount of effort required, especially when better-looking steps can be constructed from cast-concrete slabs and blocks. Nevertheless, if you have a flight of concrete steps in your garden you will want to keep them in good condition. Like other forms of masonry, concrete suffers from spalling, where frost breaks down the surface and flakes off fragments of material. It occurs a great deal along the front edges of steps where foot traffic adds to the problem. Repair broken edges as soon as you can – not only are they ugly, but the steps are not as safe as they might be.

Building up broken edges
Wearing safety goggles, chip away concrete around the damaged area and provide a good grip for fresh concrete. Cut a board to the height of the riser and prop it against the step with bricks **(1)**. Mix up a small batch of general-purpose concrete, but add a little PVA bonding agent to help it stick to the step. Dilute some bonding agent with water, say 3 parts water : 1 part bonding agent, and brush it onto the damaged area, stippling it into the crevices. When the surface becomes tacky, fill the hole with concrete mix flush with the edge of the board **(2)**. Radius the front edge slightly with a home-made edging float, running it against the board **(3)**.

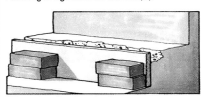

1 Prop a board against the riser

2 Fill the front edge with concrete

3 Run an edging float against the board

To build a series of curved steps, choose materials which will make the job as easy as possible. You can use tapered concrete slabs for the treads, designing the circumference of the steps to suit the proportions of the slabs. Alternatively, you can construct the treads from crazy paving, selecting fairly large stones for the front edge. Use bricks laid flat or on edge to build the risers. Set the bricks to radiate from the centre of the curve, and fill the slightly tapered joints with mortar.

Use a length of string attached to a peg driven into the ground as an improvised compass to mark out the curve of each step. Tie a batten to the string to help you gauge the front edge of the lower steps **(1)**. Roughly shape the soil and lay a concrete foundation for the bottom riser. Build risers and treads as for regular concrete-slab steps, using the improvised string compass as a guide.

Building circular landings
To construct a circular landing, build the front edge with bricks and paving as for a curved step. When the mortar has set, fill the area of the landing with compacted hardcore and lay gravel up to the level of the tread **(2)**.

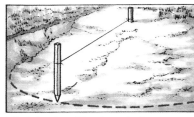

1 Mark the edge with an improvised compass

2 Circular landings made with bricks and gravel

For an informal garden, build steps from lengths of sawn timber soaked in a chemical preserver. Try to construct risers of a fairly regular height, otherwise someone might stumble if they are forced to break step. As it is not always possible to obtain uniform logs you may have to make up the height of the riser with two or more slimmer logs.

Cut a regular slope in the earth bank and compact the soil by treading it down. Drive stakes cut from 75mm (3in) diameter logs into the ground, one at each end of a step **(1)**. Place one heavy log behind the stakes, bedding it down in the soil **(2)**, and pack hardcore behind it to construct the tread of the step **(3)**. Shovel a layer of gravel on top of the hardcore to finish the step.

If large logs are in short supply, build a step from two or three slim logs, holding them against the stakes with hardcore as you construct the riser **(4)**.

Log-built garden steps

1 Drive a stake at each end of a step

2 Place a log behind the stakes

3 Fill behind the log with hardcore

4 Make up a riser with two slim logs

There is nothing like still or running water to enliven a garden. Waterfalls and fountains have an almost mesmeric fascination and the sound of trickling water has a delightfully soothing effect. Even a small area of still water will support all manner of interesting pond life and plants, with the additional bonus of the images of trees, rocks and sky reflected in its placid surface.

Pond liners

It is not by chance that the number of garden ponds has greatly increased over recent years; their popularity is largely due to the emergence of easily installed rigid and flexible pond liners, making it possible to create a complete water garden by putting in just a few days' work.

In the past it was necessary to line a pond with concrete. While it is true that concrete is a very versatile material, there is always the possibility of a leak developing through cracks caused by ground movement or the force of expanding ice. There are no such worries with rigid and flexible liners. In addition to the labour and expense involved in building formers for a concrete pond, it must be left to season for about a month, during which time it must be emptied and refilled a number of times to ensure that the water will be safe for fish and plant life. However, you can introduce plants to a pool lined with plastic or rubber as soon as the water itself has matured, which takes no more than a few days.

Ordering a flexible liner

Use a simple formula to calculate the size of liner you will need. Disregard the design, planting shelves and so on that you have planned; simply take the overall length and width of the pond and add twice the maximum depth to each dimension to arrive at the size of the liner. If possible, adapt your design to fall within the nearest stock liner size.

POND DIMENSIONS	
Length – 3m	9ft 9in
Width – 2m	6ft 6in
Depth – 450mm	1ft 6in
SIZE OF LINER	
3m + 0.900m = 3.9m	9ft 9in + 3ft = 12ft 9in
2m + 0.900m = 2.9m	6ft 6in + 3ft = 9ft 9in

Garden pond
A well-planted water garden surrounded by flowering shrubs looks like a natural pond.

CHOOSING A POND LINER

The advantages of proprietary pond liners over concrete are fairly clear, but there are still a number of options to choose from, depending on the size and shape of the pond you wish to create and how much you propose to spend.

Rigid liners

Regular garden-centre visitors will be familiar with the range of preformed plastic pond liners. The best liners are those made from rigid glass-reinforced plastic (fibreglass), which is very strong and resistant to the effects of frost or ice. Provided they are handled with a reasonable degree of care and installed correctly, rigid plastic pond liners are practically leak-proof.

Semi-rigid liners

Semi-rigid liners, made from vacuum-formed plastic, are cheaper than those made from fibreglass, but the range of sizes is very limited. However, they make ideal reservoirs or header pools for the top of a cascade or waterfall.

Rectangular or irregular-shaped liners are available in rigid or semi-rigid plastic, and a very acceptable water garden can be created with a carefully selected series of pond liners linked together by watercourses.

Flexible liners

For complete freedom of design, choose a flexible-sheet liner designed to hug the contours of a pond of virtually any shape and size. Another advantage is that a pond made with even the most expensive sheet liner is cheaper to construct than a rigid-plastic liner of equivalent size; it is also guaranteed to last longer.

Polyethylene liners, once the only type of flexible liner on the market, are relatively fragile and should be considered only for temporary pools; even then, they should be lined with a double thickness of material. PVC liners, especially those reinforced with nylon, are guaranteed for up to 10 years of normal use, but if you want your pond to last for 50 years or more, choose a synthetic-rubber membrane based on butyl. Not all butyl liners are of the same quality, so buy one from a reputable manufacturer offering a 20-year written guarantee if you want the best product. Black and stone-coloured butyl liners are made in a wide range of stock sizes up to 6.5 x 10.75m (22 x 35ft); larger liners can be supplied to order.

Rigid pond liner
Rigid liners are moulded using glass-reinforced plastic.

Flexible liners
The better-quality flexible liners are made from butyl.

57

DESIGNING A POND

A pond must be sited correctly if it is to have any chance of maturing into an attractive, clear stretch of water. Never place a pond under deciduous trees – falling leaves will pollute the water as they decay, causing fish to become ill and even die. Laburnum trees are especially poisonous.

Positioning for sunlight
Although sunlight promotes the growth of algae, which causes ponds to turn a pea-green colour, it is also necessary to encourage the growth of other water plants. An abundant growth of oxygenating plants will compete with the algae for mineral salts and, aided by shade cast from floating and marginal plants, will keep the pond clear.

Size and shape
The proportion of the pond is important in creating harmony between plants and fish. It is difficult to maintain the right conditions for clear water in a pond less than 3.75sq m (40sq ft) in surface area, but the volume of water is even more vital. A pond up to about 9sq m (100sq ft) in area should be 450mm (1ft 6in) deep. As the area increases you will have to dig deeper to about 600mm (2ft) or more, but it's rarely necessary to go below 750mm (2ft 6in).

The profile of the pond must be designed to fulfil certain requirements. To grow marginal plants, you will need a 225mm (9in) wide shelf around the edge of the pond, 225mm (9in) below the surface of the water. This will take a standard 150mm (6in) planting crate with ample water above, and you can always raise the crate on pieces of paving or bricks. The sides of the pond should slope at about 20 degrees to prevent soil collapse during construction and to allow the liner to stretch without promoting too many creases. It will also allow a sheet of ice to float upwards without damaging the liner. Judge the angle by measuring 75mm (3in) inwards for every 225mm (9in) of depth. If the soil is very sandy, increase the angle of slope slightly for extra stability.

Accommodating a sloping site
On a sloping site build up the low side with earth, turfing up to the paving surround. Cut back the higher side and build a low retaining wall, or bed stones against the earth to create a rockery.

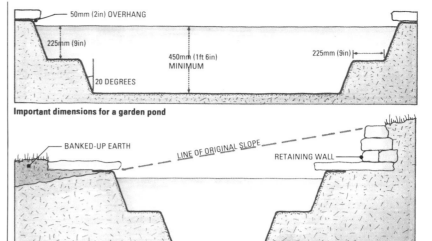

Important dimensions for a garden pond

Accommodating a sloping site

Installing a rigid liner

Stand a rigid liner in position and prop it up with cardboard boxes, both to check its orientation and to mark its perimeter on the ground. Use a spirit level to plot key points on the ground (1) and mark them with small pegs. You will need to dig outside this line, so absolute accuracy is not required.

As you move the topsoil, either take it away in a wheelbarrow or pile it close by, ready to incorporate into a rockery. Lay a straightedge across the top and measure the depth of the excavation (2), including marginal shelves. Keep the excavation as close as possible to the shape of the liner, but extend it by 150mm (6in) on all sides. Compact the base and cover it with a 25mm (1in)

deep level of sharp sand. Lower the liner and bed it firmly into the sand. Check that the pool stands level (3) and wedge it temporarily with wooden battens until the back-fill of soil or sand can hold it.

Start to fill the liner with water from a hose and, at the same time, pour sifted soil or sand behind the liner (4). There is no need to hurry as it will take some time to fill, but keep pace with the level of the water. Reach into the excavation and pack soil under the marginal shelves with your hands.

When the liner is firmly bedded in the soil, either finish the edge with stones as for a flexible liner (see opposite) or re-lay turf to cover the rim of the liner.

1 Mark the perimeter of the liner

2 Measure the depth of the excavation

3 Make sure the liner stands level

4 Infill with sifted soil or sand

CONSTRUCTING A POND: FLEXIBLE LINER

Excavating the pond

Mark out the shape of the pond on the ground. A garden hose is useful for trying out curvilinear shapes. Excavate the pond to the level of the planting shelf, then mark and dig out the deeper sections (1). Remove sharp stones and roots from the sides and base to make sure they won't puncture the liner.

The top of the pond must be level, and the surrounding stone or concrete slabs must be 18mm (¾in) below the turf. For both reasons, cut back the turf to accommodate the stones and then drive wooden datum pegs into the exposed surround every metre or so (3 to 4 ft). Level the tops of all the pegs using a straightedge (2) and check the level across the pond as well. Remove or pack earth around the pegs until the compacted soil is level below the pegs.

When the surround is level, remove the pegs and spread a 12mm (½in) layer of slightly damp sand over the base and sides of the excavations (3).

Installing a flexible liner

Drape the liner across the excavation with an even overlap all round and hold it in place with bricks while you fill the pond with water from a hose (4). It will take several hours to fill a large pond, but check it regularly, moving the bricks as the liner stretches. A few creases are inevitable around sharp curves, but you will lose most of them by keeping the liner fairly taut and easing it into shape as the water rises. Turn off the water when the level reaches 50mm (2in) below the edge of the pond. Cut off surplus liner with scissors, leaving a 150mm (6in) overlap all round (5). Push 100mm (4in) nails through the overlap into the soil so that the liner cannot slip while you place the edging stones.

Building the surround

Lay flat stones dry at first, selecting those which follow the shape of the pond with a reasonably close fit between them. Let the stones project over the water by about 50mm (2in) to cast a deep shadow line and reflection. Using a bolster, cut stones to fit the gaps behind the larger edging stones. Lift the stones one or two at a time and bed them on two or three strategically placed mounds of mortar mixed with 1 part cement : 3 parts soft sand (6). Tap the stones level with a mallet and fill the joints with a trowel. Smooth the joints flush with an old paintbrush. Do not drop mortar in the water or you will have to empty and refill the pond before you introduce fish or plants.

INCORPORATING A DRAIN

The recommended water level for a pond is about 50mm (2in) below the edging stones, but in exceptional circumstances, such as a heavy storm, or if you forget to turn off the water when topping up, the water can rise fast enough to spill over and flood the garden. As a precaution, build a drain beneath the edging stones to allow excess water to escape; this will also provide a means of running electric cable into the pond to power a pump or lighting. Cut corrugated-plastic sheet into two strips 150mm (6in) wide and long enough to run under the edging stones. Pop-rivet the strips together to make a channel about 25mm (1in) deep (1). Scrape earth and sand from beneath the liner to accommodate the channel (2), then lay edging stones on top to hold it in place. Dig a small soakaway behind the channel and fill it with rubble topped with fine gravel or turf up to the level of the stones.

2 Place finished drain beneath edging stones

● **Preventing punctures**
A cushion of sand normally prevents a pool liner being punctured, but on very stony ground it pays to install additional protection in the form of polyester matting, which is available from garden centres.

1 Dig the excavation as accurately as possible

2 Level the edge using datum pegs

3 Line the excavation with damp sand

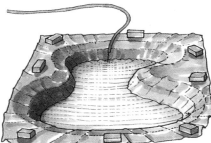

4 Stretch the liner by filling the pond

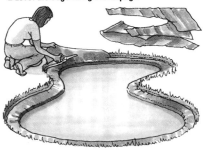

5 Cut the flexible liner to fit

6 Lay edging stones to complete the pond

MAKING A RAISED-EDGE POND

If you want a more formal pond you can build a raised edge using bricks or concrete facing blocks. An edging about 450mm (1ft 6in) high serves as a deterrent for small children while also providing seating. If you prefer a low wall, say 225mm (9in) high, create planting shelves at ground level, digging the pond deeper in the centre. Place planting crates on blocks around the edge of a deep raised pond.

Building the pond

Lay 100 to 150mm (4 to 6in) concrete footings to support the walls, which are constructed from two skins of masonry set apart to match the width of flat coping stones. Allow for an overhang of 50mm (2in) over the water's edge and lap the outer wall by 12 to 18mm (½ to ¾in). To save money, build the inner wall from plain concrete blocks or cheap common bricks, reserving more expensive decorative bricks or facing blocks for the outer skin of the wall. Raised ponds can be lined with a standard flexible liner, or you can order a prefabricated fitted liner to reduce the amount of creasing at the corners. Trap the edge of the liner underneath the coping stones.

Raised-edge pond
A well-designed and well-constructed pond which is attractively integrated into a sloping site.

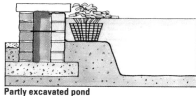

Partly excavated pond

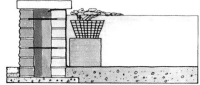

Fully raised pond built with a cavity wall

ALTERNATIVE POND EDGING

Edging a pond with flat stones provides a safe and attractive footpath for tending to water plants and fish, but a more natural setting is often required, particularly for small header pools in a rockery. Incorporate a shelf around the pond as for marginal plants, but this time for an edging of rocks. If you place them carefully there is no need to mortar them. Arrange rocks behind the edging to cover the liner (**1**).

To create a shallow, beach-like edging, slope the soil at a very shallow angle and lay large pebbles or flat rocks upon the liner. You can merge them with a rockery or let them form a natural water line (**2**).

To discourage neighbourhood cats poaching fish from a pond, create an edging of trailing plants. Without a firm foothold, no cat will attempt to reach into the water. Bed a strip of soft wire netting in the mortar below flat edging stones. Cut the strip to overhang the water by about 150mm (6in) as a support for the plants (**3**). Once the plants are established they will disguise the nature of the pool liner.

1 Rock-edged pond

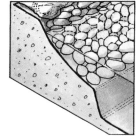

2 Pebble-strewn shelf

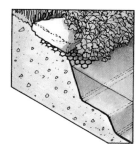

3 Wire edge holds plants

Pumps and fountains

Small submersible pumps for fountains and waterfalls are operated either directly from the mains electrical supply or through a transformer which reduces the voltage to 24 volts. Mains electricity and water can be fatal, so consult a qualified electrician if you plan to use a mains-operated pump. An extra-low-voltage pump is perfectly safe and can be installed and wired simply.

Place the pump in the water and run its electric cable beneath the edging stones, preferably via a homemade drain, to a waterproof connector attached to the extension lead of a transformer installed inside the house. This permits removal of the pump for servicing without disturbing the extension cable or transformer. Run the pump regularly, even in the winter, to keep it in good working order, and clean both the pump and its filter according to the manufacturer's instructions.

There are so many waterfall pumps and fountain kits available that you should consult manufacturers' catalogues to find one that best suits your purpose. Place a submersible waterfall pump close to the edge of the pond so that you can reach it to disconnect the hose running to the waterfall when you need to service the pump. Stand fountain units on a flat stone or propped up on bricks so that the jet is vertical. Plant water lilies some distance away from a fountain as falling water will encourage the flowers to close up.

Extra-low-voltage waterfall pump and transformer

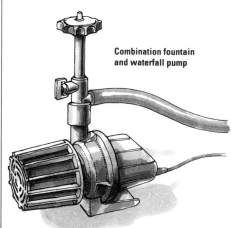

Combination fountain and waterfall pump

A waterfall, complemented by a rockery planted with alpines or graceful shrubs and trees such as Japanese maple or dwarf conifers, adds a further dimension to a water garden. The technique for building a series of watercourses is not as complicated as it may appear, and at the same time you can also cover much of the groundwork needed for your rockery.

Materials

You will be surprised at the amount of soil produced by excavating a pond. To avoid waste and the trouble of transporting it to a local dump, use it to create your pool-side rockery. If you include a small reservoir on the higher ground you can pump water into it from the main pond to be returned via a trickling waterfall.

Obtaining a sufficient number of stones to give the impression of a real rocky outcrop can work out extremely expensive if you buy them from a garden centre. A cheaper way is to use hollow-cast reproduction rocks, which will eventually weather-in quite well. However, your best option is to buy natural stone direct from a local quarry. Real rocks can be very heavy, so have them delivered as close to the site as possible and hire a strong trolley to facilitate moving individual stones about the garden.

A rockery and waterfall are built as one operation, but for the sake of clarity they are described separately here.

BUILDING A ROCKERY AND WATERFALL

SEE ALSO

Details for:
Obtaining stone   24
Pond liners   57

Creating a waterfall

So that the waterfall can discharge directly into the main pond, form a small inlet at the side of the pond by leaving a large flap of flexible liner. Build shallow banks at each side of the inlet and line it with stones (1). Create a stepped watercourse ascending in stages to the reservoir. Line the watercourse with off-cuts of flexible liner, overlapping them on the face of each waterfall. Tuck the edge of each lower piece of liner under the edge of the piece above, and hold them in place with stones. To retain water in small pools along the watercourse, cut each step with a slope towards the rear (2) and place stones along the lip for the desired effect (3). A flat stone will produce a sheet of water, a layer of pebbles a rippling cascade.

As the construction work progresses, test the watercourse by running water from a garden hose as it is difficult to adjust the angle of stones once the watercourse has been completed.

Bury the flexible hose from the waterfall pump in the rockery, making sure there are no sharp bends which would restrict the flow of water. Cut the hose so that it emerges at the edge of the reservoir and cover it with a flat stone (4) to hold and hide it.

A rigid-plastic reservoir will have a lip moulded in one edge which allows water to escape down the watercourse. If you construct a reservoir with flexible liner, however, you will have to shape the edge to form a low point and support a flat stone over the opening to hide the liner (5).

Cascades and waterfalls

This cross section shows a series of cascades and waterfalls running from reservoir to pond.
1 Pond inlet.
2 Watercourse step.
3 Overhanging stone creates a sheet of water.
4 Hose from pump.
5 Reservoir outlet.
6 Reservoir.

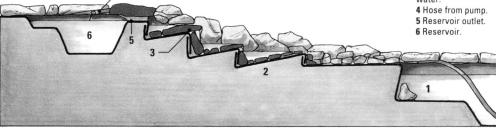

Constructing a rockery

Select and place each stone in a rockery to create an illusion of layers of rock. Stones placed haphazardly at odd angles tend to resemble a spoil heap rather than a natural outcrop. Take care not to strain yourself when lifting rocks. Keep your feet together and use your leg muscles to do the work, keeping your back as straight as possible. To move a particularly heavy rock, slip a rope around it (see left).

Lay large, flat rocks to form the front edge of the rockery, placing soil behind

and between them to form a flat, level platform. Compact the soil to make sure there are no air pockets which will damage the roots of plants. Lay subsequent layers of rock set back from the first, but not in a regular pattern. Place some to create steep embankments, others to form a gradual slope of wide steps. Pockets of soil for planting alpines or other small rockery plants will form naturally as you lay the stones, but plan larger areas of soil for specimen shrubs or dwarf trees.

Building a rockery
A rockery should have irregular rock 'steps' along its front edge.

Lifting stones
Keep your back straight when lifting heavy stones (right). Use a rope to lift and place large rocks (below).

Incorporating a bog garden

An area of wet, boggy soil where specialized waterside plants can flourish complements a pond perfectly. When you excavate the pond, make a wide planting shelf covered with the flexible liner. Place a row of stones to form the edge of the pond, dividing the bog area from the deep water. Bed the stones in 50mm (2in) of mortar. When the mortar has set, neutralize its lime content by painting on a solution of

waterproofing powder available from pond specialists. Follow the manufacturer's instructions for its use.

Incorporate the bog garden into a rockery by lining the perimeter with stones, then fill the area with soil. The liner underneath the soil will retain sufficient moisture to keep the garden permanently damp, but make the planting bed deep enough to ensure that the plants will not be waterlogged.

BOG GARDEN

POND

Bog garden
Construct a bog garden next to a pond for waterside plants.

CHOOSING A SWIMMING POOL

SEE ALSO
Details for:
Official approval   72-73

Owning a private swimming pool is no longer the exclusive privilege of the rich and famous. Several specialist companies offer reasonably priced pool kits which you can install yourself. It is worth hiring professional help for deep excavations and to remove soil from the site, and anything but the most basic heating equipment should be installed by a qualified tradesperson. Most authorities do not insist on planning permission for the building of a private pool in your garden, but it is required if you erect an enclosure over the pool. Once a pool is filled it requires very little water for topping up and maintenance, but you may find it advantageous to have a water meter fitted by your local water authority prior to the installation of your swimming pool.

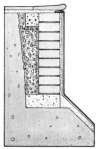

Sunken-pool kits
Vinyl liners are used with block-built walls or a frame-and-panel construction.

Block-wall construction

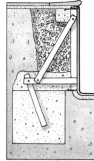

Frame-and-panel walling

● **Tiled concrete pools**
For a top-quality permanent pool, hire a professional contractor to install a reinforced-concrete structure. Hollow pool walls, constructed with cast-concrete sections, are filled with vibrated concrete, rendered and lined with polished marble or mosaic tiles.

A self-assembly pool
Swimming pools made from self-assembly kits are just as attractive as professionally installed pools, but are a fraction of the cost.

Siting a swimming pool

The size and shape of a swimming pool is largely dictated by the area of your garden, but it should be positioned away from trees so that it benefits from the sun and does not collect falling leaves. Most people prefer to install a pool reasonably close to the house so that the facilities of the latter can be used to supply water, electricity and heating, and an existing building such as a garage can be utilized to house the pool filtration plant. It is normally easier to install a pool on a level site, but you can partially bury one in a sloping bank and fill in the lower area with the excavated soil.

Above-ground pool kits

Above-ground pools are cheap and easy to erect. Most are circular or oval in plan, and are constructed by bolting together galvanized-steel panels and frame members. A heavy-duty vinyl liner and wide coping strips complete the basic pool. Above-ground pools are the least likely to be contaminated by wind-blown leaves and other debris, and they can be dismantled and moved when you buy another house. Young children cannot fall into the water once you have removed the steps. With some modification you can partially bury an above-ground pool and bank the excavated soil around the sides.

Sunken-pool kits

Sunken pools can be built in a wide range of shapes and sizes from prefabricated panels similar to those used for above-ground pools. The wall panels, anchored in concrete, line the perimeter of the pool to a depth of about 1m (3ft 3in). A deeper hopper-shaped excavation at one end of the pool is rendered with a sand-and-cement mix before a fitted vinyl liner is installed. The pool walls are back-filled with gravel to balance the water pressure, and an edging of shaped coping stones is bedded in mortar. Similar pools are built using standard concrete blocks laid on a concrete footing to construct the walls. The walls and floor are rendered to present a smooth face to the vinyl liner. You could hire a local builder to construct and render the walls and floor, then back-fill and line the pool yourself.

A swimming-pool liner will last for years but, should one become damaged accidentally, it can be patched without emptying the pool.

SWIMMING-POOL ACCESSORIES

Some accessories, such as diving boards, water chutes and underwater lights, merely add to your enjoyment of the pool. Others are absolutely essential to keep the water pure.

Skimmer and filter
A pump-operated skimmer built into the side of a pool sucks lightweight floating debris into a filter housed outside the pool. The filtered water is returned to the pool via a separate inlet. The entire unit is supplied with most pool kits.

Pool vacuum cleaner
You will need a special vacuum cleaner to remove the heavier debris that sinks to the bottom of the pool. Its hose connects to the pool-side skimmer.

Leaf net
Buy a net attached to a long pole to periodically remove floating leaves which might clog the filter.

Pool cover
Lightweight woven covers are available for both above-ground and sunken pools to keep leaves, twigs and other windblown debris out of the water during the winter months.

Test equipment
Chlorine or other chemicals must be added to the water at regular intervals to kill harmful bacteria and algae. The water must be analysed in order to maintain an effective chemical balance. Pool kits are supplied with simple test equipment which allows you to analyse water samples yourself.

Heating the water
Floating thermal blankets, which are removed prior to swimming, provide the cheapest means of raising the water temperature. They are essential to reduce the cost of heating the water by more sophisticated equipment. You can install a heat exchanger which uses heat produced by the house central-heating boiler or a separate boiler provided exclusively for the pool, although both methods are expensive. Solar panels or mats provide free heat, but installation costs are high. A heat pump which extracts heat from the surrounding air, even during a cloudy day, is probably the most effective way to heat a swimming pool.

CONSERVATORIES

Ever since the Victorian well-to-do used them to raise exotic plants and relax in, conservatories have been a desirable addition to any house. Today, with double glazing and efficient modern heating, they are used to extend the home to provide not only an indoor garden, but living and dining rooms, studios, workrooms and sometimes kitchens. Conservatories are made in a wide range of standard sizes and styles. They are available in kit form for self-build or are supplied and erected for you.

The materials used for the construction of conservatories may include traditional softwood framing combined with dwarf masonry walls, hardwood timber frames and panels, or aluminium or uPVC plastic framing in traditional and modern styles. The roof may use traditional glass panes or modern double or triple-wall polycarbonate plastic sheet. Double-glazed toughened-glass sealed units are generally used for the windows and doors.

Study the range of designs to choose a conservatory that will suit the style of the house. A decorative 'Victorian-style' conservatory will be acceptable for an ornate or period house but may look out of place with a modern one. However, a plain modern-style conservatory can sometimes look at home with an old house. The proportions of the design and the quality of the building materials and construction details are important factors to consider.

From a practical point of view, traditional softwood frames will need periodic painting and hardwood frames occasional treatment with a coloured wood preserver. Aluminium frames are factory finished and like uPVC conservatories should require little or no decorative maintenance.

The period style of the conservatory complements the character of the house

Choosing the site

Although formal planning permission and Building Regulation approval are usually not required for conservatories under 30sq m (323sq ft) in most areas, it is sensible to discuss your proposed development with the local authorities. Before committing to your preferred design, check the manufacturer's specification to establish the size of the conservatory in relation to your site, any problems with drainage and possibly the proximity of trees or other garden features. Quite apart from practical matters, which can also include the ease of access from the house and ventilation, the choice of location should also take into consideration the direction of the sun.

A conservatory built on a south-facing wall will benefit from available sunshine all year round and would provide a pleasant environment in the winter months. However, in high summer it will be hot and will require good ventilation and shading to be comfortable. A west-facing conservatory will provide a bright room which will receive less direct sunlight and be comfortable to sit in during the afternoons and evenings. East-facing conservatories will catch only the morning sunlight. A north-facing one will not receive direct sunlight and for much of the winter require efficient heating while providing an attractive, comfortable environment in the summer. If you use a corner site your options are increased.

Heating and ventilation

Conservatories are particularly susceptible to changes in the elements and need to have a controlled environment if they are not to be too hot in summer and cold in winter. The large expanse of glass will quickly absorb the natural heat from the sun but can equally quickly lose any heat in cold wintery weather.

Double glazing is essential to retain the heat gained from sunlight, particularly if the conservatory is to be used all year round. Ideally low-emissivity glass should be used, as this reflects the absorbed heat back into the room. However in winter months when the sun's rays are weak and outside temperatures are usually low it will be necessary to provide internal heating. This is usually provided by an extension to the house central-heating system or electric-powered heaters.

In high summer the heat can rise to uncomfortable levels. To help overcome this fit blinds at the windows and to the underside of the roof. Special heat-reflective types are available. These not only add shade and an elegant finish to the interior, they also contribute to reducing heat loss in winter. Conservatory suppliers can provide made-to-measure blinds to fit your particular requirements.

However effective blinds may be, it is essential to have good ventilation, not only to combat heat in summer but also to reduce condensation in winter. Most conservatories are supplied with opening windows or top vents, and roof ventilators, to provide cross-ventilation. Roof ventilators are normally manually operated but temperature-controlled automatic systems are available as optional extras.

BUILDING CONSERVATORIES

Although conservatories are relatively light structures it is essential that a suitable base is constructed. Erecting one on an existing patio is unlikely to be acceptable. Suppliers will specify a typical base for their products, but as site conditions can vary you should consult your local Building Control Officer. Problems associated with the base covering underfloor ventilation, the level of the DPC, or drains running below the base may also need to be discussed. A concrete base is usually recommended, but a special metal-frame platform that requires less site preparation may be a possible alternative.

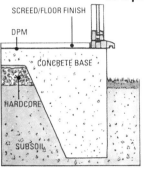

1 Concrete raft conservatory base

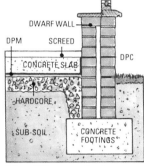

2 Trenchfill conservatory base

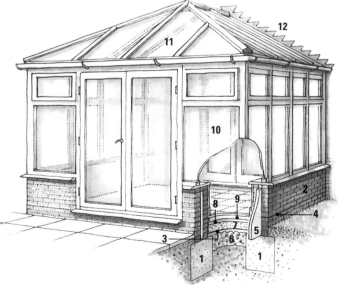

Components of a conservatory

1 Concrete footings
2 Dwarf cavity wall
3 Damp-proof membrane
4 Damp-proof course
5 Cavity insulation
6 Blinded hardcore
7 Concrete slab
8 Insulation board
9 Sand-and-cement screed
10 Double glazed frames
11 Hipped glazed roof
12 Flashing

Types of concrete base

A typical base specification has a 100mm (4in) thick slab of concrete, which may or may not be screeded, laid over a minimum of 100mm (4in) of well compacted hardcore and with adequately deep footings to suit the ground conditions. This can be constructed as a concrete raft which combines the footings (1), or more often, a trenchfill concrete foundation supporting masonry walls which contain the concrete slab (2).

The base must incorporate a continuous damp-proof membrane and a damp-proof course that is linked into the house DPC.

Constructing a base

A typical trenchfill type is described here. Start by marking out with chalk the finished floor level on the house wall. Using profile boards, set out the area of the base foundations following closely the dimensions given by the conservatory manufacturer. Check the house wall is vertical with a plumb bob held at side-frame height. If it leans outwards, set the base dimensions from the plumb line, not the wall.

The width of the footings should be 300mm (1ft) for a wall of single-brick construction, or 450mm (1ft 6in) for a cavity wall with a 50mm (2in) cavity. A minimum depth of 500mm (1ft 8in) set two or three brick courses below ground level should be suitable for most sites. Dig out the trenches and pour in concrete to the required level.

Excavate the area within the footings to allow for the thickness of the floor covering, floor screed, concrete slab, insulation board if required, and sand-blinded hardcore. Lay the perimeter bricks up to at least 150mm (6in) above ground level. Lay a bedding of well compacted hardcore in the excavation and cover with up to 50mm (2in) of levelled sand. Lay a polyethylene DPM over the sand with the edges of the sheet overlapping the walls all round (the inner skin of a cavity wall), and turned up the house wall at the back. Insulation board can now be laid (see right). Lay the concrete slab to a minimum of 100mm (4in).

Lay a damp-proof course on the walls and tie it into the house DPC, then complete the brickwork. Finally, after erecting the framing, complete the base by laying a sand-and-cement screed followed by the floor covering when fully dry. If flooring panels are to be laid over insulation boards the screed can be omitted.

Erecting the frame

It is essential the sill is set level and the modular frames are mounted squarely.

Erect the frame units following the detailed instructions provided by the manufacturer. Any gaps at the junctions with the house wall should be filled with silicone mastic. The roof wall rafter should also be sealed and covered with flashing. A traditional lead flashing or a self-adhesive type can be used. The flashing should be tucked into a mortar joint or a groove cut in the wall about 100mm (4in) to 150mm (6in) up the wall and pointed or filled with mastic. The lower edge should be dressed over the top edge of the wall rafter.

If the conservatory is built against a cavity wall that is subjected to driving rain it may be necessary to fit cavity trays into the wall above the roof line prior to erecting the frame.

INSULATING A BASE

The Building Regulations require a new floor to be insulated, but this does not apply for a conservatory under 30sq m (323sq ft) unless it is used as a habitable room. However it would be sensible to include insulation in any case as it will help conserve energy.

Expanded-polystyrene insulation board can be incorporated in the base or laid over it. The extra thickness of the insulation, up to 50mm (2in), will need to be taken into account when excavating the ground for the concrete slab.

For a screeded floor the insulation can be placed under the concrete slab (1), or under a screed not less than 65mm (2½in) thick (2). The insulation in either case is turned up the wall to prevent cold bridging.

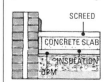

1 Insulation under concrete slab

2 Insulation under screed

Just a few outdoor light fittings can transform a garden dramatically. Spot or floodlights can emphasize particularly attractive features, at the same time providing functional lighting for pathways and steps, while strings of light bulbs woven through foliage afford attractive background illumination. The most impressive effects are produced with underwater lights, which can make small pools or fountains the focal points of a garden.

Extra-low-voltage lighting
A number of garden light fittings can be powered directly from mains electricity, though they need to be installed by a professional electrician. However, you can install light fittings or a complete lighting kit yourself if they connect up to an extra-low-voltage transformer.

Store the transformer under cover in a garage or workshop, close to a 13amp socket outlet, and connect it to the socket by an ordinary square-pin plug. The flex, which is normally supplied with the light fitting, is connected to the two 12 volt outlet terminals on the transformer. Carry out the connections to the lights following the instructions supplied by the manufacturer.

Unless the makers state otherwise, extra-low-voltage flex supplying garden lights can be run along the ground without further protection, but inspect it regularly and don't let it trail over stone steps or other sharp edges that could damage the PVC insulation if someone steps on it. If you have to add extra flex, use a waterproof connector.

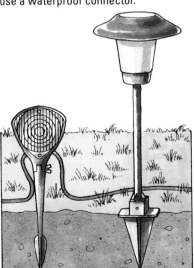
Typical extra-low-voltage garden light fittings

Pool lighting

Pool lights are normally submerged so as to have at least 18mm (¾in) of water above their lenses. Some are designed to float unless they are held below the surface by smooth stones placed carefully on the flex.

Submerged lights get covered by the particles of debris that float in all ponds. To clean the lenses without removing the lights from the water, simply direct a gentle hose over them.

Occasionally you will have to remove a light and wash the lens thoroughly in warm soapy water. Always disconnect the power supply before you handle the lights or take them out of the pond.

Run the flex for pool lighting under the edging stones via a drain made from corrugated plastic sheeting. The entire length of the flex can be protected from adverse weather by being run through a length of ordinary garden hose. Take the safest route to the power supply, anchoring the flex gently in convenient spots – but do not cover it with soil or grass in case someone inadvertently cuts through it with a spade or fork. Join lengths of low-voltage cable with waterproof connectors.

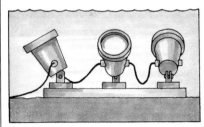
Stand underwater floodlights on a flat stone

Pumps

Electric pumps in garden pools provide fountains and waterfalls. A combination unit will send an adjustable jet of water up into the air, at the same time pumping water through a plastic tube to the top of a rockery to trickle back into the pool.

Some pumps run directly from the mains supply. To fit these, follow the manufacturer's instructions and consult an electrician. But there are also extra-low-voltage pumps that connect to a transformer shielded from the weather (see left). So you can disconnect the pump without disturbing the extra-low-voltage wiring to the transformer, join two lengths of cable with a waterproof connector. Conceal the connector under a stone or gravel beside the pool.

Most manufacturers recommend you take a pump from the water at the end of each season, clean it thoroughly, then return it to the water immediately. To avoid corrosion, don't leave it out of the water for very long without cleaning and drying it. Never service a pump without first disconnecting it from the power supply. During the winter, run the pump for an hour every week to keep it in good working condition.

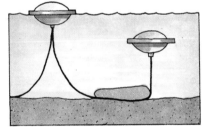
Place a stone on the cable to submerge a light

SEE ALSO
Details for:
Pond drain   59

● **Extra-low-voltage**
This is the strictly correct term to describe equipment that runs on 50V or less. However, manufacturers and suppliers often use the term low-voltage to describe similar equipment.

Waterproof cable connector
A suitable cable connector is available from pump and lighting suppliers.

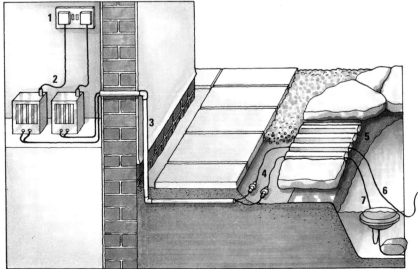

Pump and lighting circuits
1 Socket outlet
2 BS3535 Type 3 isolating transformers
3 Plastic conduit
4 Waterproof connectors
5 Home-made drain
6 Pump cable
7 Lighting cable

WOODWORM
ATTACK

SEE ALSO
Details for:
Preservers 70

Our homes and surroundings are sometimes invaded by voracious insect pests. Some of them are quite harmless, although they cause a great deal of annoyance and even alarm, but certain insects can severely weaken the structure of a building and they often go unnoticed until the damage is done. At the first signs of infestation, try to identify and eradicate the pests as quickly as possible – before they seriously damage your home.

Attack by woodworm

Furniture beetle
Woodworm is the term used to describe all kinds of wood-boring insects.

The most common of these pests is the furniture beetle. The adult insect is a brown beetle about 3mm (⅛in) long, but the damage is caused by its larvae, which feed on the sapwood of most household timbers. The beetle, which is most active in early summer, lays its eggs in the crevices of bare timber. When the grubs hatch, they burrow into the wood for up to three years, then pupate just below the surface. The new adult emerges by chewing its way out, leaving the familiar round flight hole. These tiny holes are about 1 to 2mm (¹⁄₁₆in) in diameter and are generally the first signs of infestation, but there may be several generations of woodworm active inside the timber.

Other types of woodworm
The furniture beetle is said to inhabit about three-quarters of British homes – and most outbreaks of woodworm are certainly caused by this pest. However, there are other wood-boring insects that can create even greater damage.

The deathwatch and house longhorn beetles bore much larger holes – from 3 to 6mm (⅛ to ¼in) in diameter. Authorities are anxious to control the spread of these rarer insects, so contact your local Environmental Health Department if you suspect their presence in your home. Another common insect pest is the weevil, which attacks wood at two stages in its life cycle. Both the adults and the grubs burrow into all types of timber – but only when it is already decaying and in a very moist condition.

Locating woodworm
Check the unfinished parts of your furniture, particularly plywood drawer bottoms and backs of cabinets, as woodworm has a taste for the glues used in their manufacture. The wooden frames of upholstered furniture are another favourite habitat of the pest; so is any form of wickerwork.

The structural timbers of your house are the place where woodworm can do most harm. Inspect roof timbers, stairs, floorboards and joists. The unpainted underedges of doors and skirtings are also common breeding grounds, as is the upper edge of picture rails.

Where the flight holes are dark in colour, the timber may have received treatment already; but clean holes, especially when surrounded by the fine dust known as frass, are signs of recent activity. If the signs are extensive, push a knife blade into the infected timbers. If the wood crumbles, the infestation is serious and you should seek the advice of a specialist contractor immediately, as the woodwork needs to be cut away and replaced. You can, nevertheless, treat basically sound timber yourself.

Wood-boring insects
(Not to scale)
These can destroy the timbers and furniture in your home. Eradicate immediately!

Furniture beetle

Deathwatch beetle

House longhorn beetle

Weevil

A typical example of woodworm attack

Inject fluid into flight holes

Treating woodworm

If woodworm is located by a surveyor when inspecting a house that you are thinking of buying, a mortgage company will insist that you hire a reputable specialist to eradicate the pest, since their work carries a 30-year guarantee. Similarly, if you detect woodworm in your present home it is wise at least to have it inspected by a specialist firm who will advise you on the extent of the damage (which may not be obvious to the untrained eye) and quote a price for treating the infested timber. There is normally no charge for this service.

Any but the most serious infestation can be treated easily, using a chemical insecticidal eradicator. Most of these fluids are flammable; so don't smoke when applying them, and extinguish any naked lights. Wear strong protective gloves and, while you are spraying the timbers, a respirator and goggles. The initial smell of solvent-based fluid can be unpleasant, but it will gradually fade.

Water-based low-odour woodworm eradicators are solvent-free and non-flammable. These eradicators will do little harm to building materials such as bitumen and expanded polystyrene, and are also suitable for use in bat roosts.

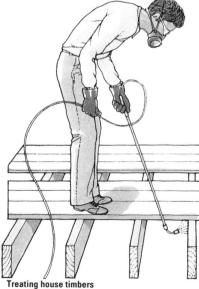
Spray fluid into confined spaces

Treating house timbers
Hire a spray lance and compressor to treat woodworm in structural timbers. Lift several floorboards and use the lance to treat the joists and undersides of the boards. Spray the boards you have removed before replacing them.

SEE ALSO
Details for:
Aluminium sealer　　77

Dealing with a minor outbreak

Treating woodworm in furniture is a fairly simple task. Use either a can with a pointed nozzle or a special aerosol applicator to inject woodworm fluid into the flight holes every 75 to 100mm (3 to 4in). As the tunnels are connected, that will be enough to penetrate deeply.

Continue the treatment by painting all unfinished timber with fluid. There's no need to paint polished surfaces, although the fluid will not harm them.

Use either a pump-action spray can or an aerosol to coat wickerwork or the inside of confined spaces.

After treatment, flight holes can be filled with cellulose filler; or use wax crayons to match the colour of show-wood. Melt the wax into a tin, and then press it into the holes with a filling knife.

Treating structural timbers

It's possible to treat timbers by flooding on the fluid using a brush, but it's more effective to spray them. Hire a sprayer that will produce a coarse spray; you will also need an extended lance in order to reach under floors and up into roof timbers. Open windows to provide as much ventilation as possible.

Remove insulating material from between ceiling joists, and vacuum the dust so that the fluid can penetrate the wood. Cover the water cistern, and check that electrical wiring is sound and clipped securely.

All exposed timbers must be soaked; but take care not to leave puddles in an attic, as they might stain the ceiling below. Should this happen, let it dry and prime the stain with aluminium sealer.

To treat a floor, lift every fourth floorboard so that you can spray all the joists and the undersides of the boards. Spray the tops of the boards, as well. The timber will dry out in two to three weeks, but you shouldn't lay impervious floorcoverings for about six months.

Preventative treatment

Any new timber can be treated with a chemical preserver to prevent attack. Once dry, it can be decorated in the normal way. Furniture can be protected with an insecticidal polish – if you buy or are given an old piece of furniture, it pays to treat it with an eradicator if there are any signs of infestation, to prevent the outbreak from spreading.

If you have to lift a door off its hinges for any reason, take the opportunity to paint the bottom edge, as woodworm does not attack painted timber.

ERADICATING OTHER INSECTS PESTS

Insecticides can be dangerous if they are allowed to contaminate food (they are also harmful to honey bees), so follow the manufacturers' instructions carefully when using them to eradicate insect pests of any kind.

Ants

The common black ant will enter a house in order to forage for food. Once established, the workers follow well-defined trails. In summer, great numbers of winged ants emerge from the nest to mate, but the swarming is over in a matter of hours, and the ants themselves are harmless. If winged ants stray into the house, they can be overcome with an insecticidal spray.

To locate the nest, follow the trail of ants. It will be situated under a path, at the base of a wall, in the lawn or under a flat stone, perhaps 6m (20ft) from the house. Destroy the nest by pouring boiling water into the entrances. If this is likely to damage plants, use an insecticidal dust or spray.

Wasps

Wasps are beneficial in spring and the early summer, as they feed on garden pests; but later in the year they destroy soft fruit. They have also been known to kill bees and raid hives for honey.

Trap foraging wasps in open jam jars containing a mixture of jam, water and detergent. Flying wasps can be killed with an aerosol fly spray. You can destroy wasps at the nest by depositing insecticidal powder near and around the entrances; tie a spoon to a cane to extend your reach. Alternatively, where there is no risk of fire, you can light a smoke-generating pellet, place it in the entrance and seal the opening.

Wasps sting when they are aroused or frightened. Treat a wasp sting with a cold compress soaked in witch hazel or use an antihistamine cream or spray.

Flies

Depending on the species, flies breed in rotting vegetables, manure, and decaying meat and offal. They can carry the eggs of parasitic worms, and spread disease by leaving small black spots of vomit and excreta on foodstuffs.

Cover food, and keep refuse in a bin liner inside a garbage bin with a tight lid. Gauze screens fitted over windows and bead curtains in open doorways will help to keep flies out of the house.

An aerosol fly spray will deal with small numbers; but for swarming flies – in a roof space, for example – use an insecticidal smoke generator (available from a hardware store or chemist). Large numbers in a living room can be sucked into a vacuum cleaner; then suck up some insecticidal powder and wait for a few hours before emptying.

Cockroaches

It is fairly rare to find cockroaches in domestic buildings, but they are sometimes attracted by warmth and a ready supply of food and water. Cockroaches are unhygienic, and smell unpleasant. Being nocturnal feeders, they tend to hide during the day in crevices in walls, behind cupboards, and above all in warm places – under cookers or fridges, for example, or near heating pipes.

A serious outbreak should be dealt with by professionals, but you can lay a finely dusted barrier of insecticidal powder between suspected daytime haunts and food supplies – taking care not to sprinkle it near the food itself. Use a paintbrush to stipple powder into crevices and under skirting boards. Once you have eradicated the pests, fill cracks and gaps to prevent a return.

Silver fish

Silver fish are tapered, wingless insects about 12mm (½in) long. They like the moist conditions found in bathrooms, kitchens and cellars. You may discover them behind wallpaper (where they feed on the paste) or in bookshelves, as they also eat paper. Use an insecticidal spray or powder in these locations.

Typical household pests
(Not to scale)
The insects shown below are more of a nuisance and a health hazard than a threat to the structure of your house.

Common black ant

Wasp

Housefly

Cockroach

Silverfish

MICE, RATS AND BATS

SEE ALSO
Details for:
Spraying preservers 66-67

Domestic mouse
Not a serious threat to health, but it is an unhygienic rodent.

Common rat
A serious health risk. Seek expert advice.

Bat
Bats are completely harmless and should not be disturbed.

Rat damage to plug

Rat damage to electric cable

Rat damage to pipework

Wear protective gloves when handling poisons

Insects are not the only pests that invade buildings. Mice and rats can be a menace, especially in houses that offer plenty of underfloor runs, where they are able to live and prosper uninterrupted and find a plentiful supply of food by invading your living quarters. Mice are a nuisance, but rats present a positive health hazard; eradication is therefore essential. Bats sometimes shelter inside houses too, usually occupying the roof space. Although you may not relish sharing your home with them, they are harmless and are now protected by law.

Mice

Mice are attracted by fallen scraps of food, so the easiest remedy is to keep floors spotlessly clean. However, mice can move from house to house, through roof spaces or wall cavities and under floors, so may be difficult to eradicate. Consult your local Environmental Health Department if they persist.

You can obtain ready-poisoned bait, which should be sprinkled onto a piece of paper or card, so uneaten bait can be easily removed. Keep pets and children away from the bait. If signs of mice are still evident after three weeks, resort to traps. Humane traps capture mice alive in a cage, enabling you to deposit them elsewhere. Although less humane, you can also use spring-loaded snap-traps.

Most people do not set enough traps. If possible, position them every 2m (6ft) across mouse runs. The best place is against the skirting, facing towards the wall. Bait traps with flour, porridge oats, or chocolate moulded onto the bait hook. Dispose of the bodies by burying, burning, or flushing them down the WC.

Rats

Serious rat infestation occurs rarely in the average domestic situation, but rats can be a problem in rural and inner-city areas or near rivers, canals and docks. They can be killed with anti-coagulant poisons; but as rats are a health hazard, always contact the Environmental Health Department for expert advice.

Bats

Bats prefer to roost in uninhabited structures such as barns, caves, mines and tunnels, but occasionally they take up residence in houses. They do not present a health hazard (their droppings are dry insect skeletons), nor do they gnaw at wood or paintwork. In fact, they are an advantage in a roof space, as they feed on woodworm beetles.

Bats are becoming very rare and are now a protected species. It is illegal to kill or injure a bat, or disturb its roosting place or block its means of access. If you are alarmed by their presence, contact your local authority for advice. You must inform the same authority if you plan to spray wood preservers or insect eradicators in a roof space inhabited by bats, since certain chemicals will harm them.

If a bat should fly into a room, try to keep calm. It will avoid you if it can – and it won't become entangled in your hair, as old wives' tales suggest. Open all the doors and windows immediately, so it is able to escape. A crawling bat can be carefully picked up in gloved hands and gently put outside.

HANDLING POISONS SAFELY

Poisons designed to kill rodents are deadly to humans too, so it is vital to follow manufacturers' handling and storage instructions to the letter. Make sure poisons are always well out of reach of children, and store them where pets and other animals cannot get at them. Never store them under the kitchen sink, where they could easily be mistaken for household products, or anywhere where they might contaminate food. If poison is accidentally consumed by humans or animals, keep the container so that the poison can be readily identified by a doctor or vet. Some containers are colour-coded specifically for this purpose. Always wear protective gloves when you handle poisons and chemicals.

Rot occurs in unprotected household timbers, fences and outbuildings that are subject to damp. Fungal spores, which are always present, multiply and develop in these conditions until eventually the timber is destroyed. Fungal attack can cause serious structural damage and requires immediate attention if costly repairs are to be avoided. The two most common scourges are wet rot and dry rot.

Recognizing rot

Signs of fungal attack are easy enough to detect – but certain strains are much more damaging than others, and so it is important to be able to identify them.

Mould growth
White furry deposits or black spots on timber, plaster or wallpaper are mould growths. Usually, these are the result of condensation. When they are wiped or scraped off, the structure shows no sign of physical deterioration apart from staining. Cure the source of the damp conditions, and treat the affected area with a fungicide or a solution of 16 parts warm water : 1 part bleach.

Wet rot

Wet rot only occurs in timber that has a high moisture content. Once the cause of the moisture is eliminated, further deterioration is arrested. Wet rot often attacks the framework of doors and windows that have been neglected, allowing rainwater to penetrate joints or between brickwork and adjacent timbers. The first sign is often peeling paintwork. Stripping the paint reveals timber that is spongy when wet, but dark brown and crumbly when dry. In advanced stages the grain splits, and thin dark-brown fungal strands will be evident on the timber. Always treat wet rot as soon as practicable.

Dry rot

Once it has taken hold, dry rot is a most serious form of decay. Urgent treatment is essential. It will attack timber with a much lower moisture content than wet rot, but only in badly ventilated confined spaces indoors – unlike wet rot, which thrives outdoors as well as indoors .

Dry rot exhibits different characteristics depending on the extent of its development. It spreads by sending out fine pale-grey strands in all directions (even through masonry) to infect drier timbers and will even pump water from damp wood. The rot can progress at an alarming rate. In very damp conditions, these 'tubules' are accompanied by white growths resembling cotton wool. These are known as mycelium. Once established, dry rot develops wrinkled, pancake-shaped fruiting bodies, which produce rust-coloured spores that are expelled to rapidly cover surrounding timber and masonry. Infested timber becomes brown and brittle, with cracks across and along the grain, causing it to break up into cube-like pieces. You may detect a strong, musty, mushroom-like smell, produced by the fungus.

Wet rot – treat it at the earliest opportunity.

Dry rot – urgent treatment is essential.

TREATING ROT

Dealing with wet rot
Once you have eliminated the cause of the damp, cut away and replace badly damaged wood, then paint the new and surrounding woodwork with three liberal applications of chemical wet-rot eradicator. Brush the liquid well into the joints and end grain.

Before decorating, you can apply a wood hardener to reinforce slightly damaged timbers, then six hours later use wood filler to rebuild the surface. Repaint as normal.

Paint rotted timbers with wood hardener

Dealing with dry rot
Dry rot requires more drastic action and should be treated by a specialist contractor unless the outbreak is minor and self-contained. The fungus is able to penetrate masonry, so look under the floorboards in adjacent rooms and check cavity walls for signs of rot.

Eliminate the source of dampness and ensure that there is adequate ventilation in roof spaces or under the floors by unblocking or installing air bricks. Cut out all infected timber up to at least 450mm (1ft 6in) beyond the last visible sign of rot. Chop plaster from nearby walls, following the strands. Continue for another 450mm (1ft 6in) beyond the extent of the growth. Collect all debris in plastic bags and burn it.

Use a chemical dry-rot eradicator to kill any remaining spores. Wire-brush the masonry, then apply three generous brushcoats to all timber, brickwork and plaster within 1.5m (5ft) of the infected area. An alternative method is to hire a coarse sprayer and go over the same area three times.

If a wall has been penetrated by strands of dry rot, drill regularly spaced, staggered holes into it from both sides. Angle the holes downwards, so the fluid will collect in them to saturate the wall internally. Patch holes after treatment.

Coat all replacement timbers with eradicator and immerse the end grain in a bucket of fluid for five to ten minutes. When you come to make good the wall, apply a zinc-oxychloride plaster.

PREVENTATIVE TREATMENT

Since fungal attack can be so damaging, it is well worth taking precautions to prevent it occurring. Regularly decorate and maintain doorframes and window frames (where water can easily penetrate) and seal around them with mastic. Provide proper ventilation between floors and ceilings, and also in the loft. Check and eradicate sources of damp, such as plumbing leaks; and (the most important precaution of all, perhaps) apply a chemical preserver to unprotected timbers during routine maintenance.

Looking after timberwork

Treat new and existing timbers with a chemical preserver. Brush and spray two or three applications on standing timbers, paying particular attention to joints and end grain.

Immersing timbers

Timber in contact with the ground will benefit from prolonged immersion in preserver. Stand fence posts on end in a bucket of fluid for 10 minutes. For smaller timbers, make a shallow bath from loose bricks and line it with thick polyethylene sheet. Fill the trough with preserver and immerse the timbers, weighing them down with bricks to prevent them from floating (**1**). To empty the bath, sink a bucket at one end of the trough, then remove the bricks at that end so the fluid will pour out (**2**).

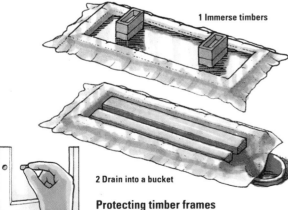

1 Immerse timbers

2 Drain into a bucket

Protecting timber frames

To protect timber frames, insert preserver in solid-tablet form into holes drilled at regular 50mm (2in) intervals in a staggered pattern. If the timber becomes wet, the tablets dissolve, placing preserver exactly where it is needed. Fill the holes with wood filler and paint as normal.

Protecting joints
Place preservative tablets close to the joints of a frame.

WOOD PRESERVERS

Water-based preservers are odourless and can safely be used on horticultural timbers. Most modern solvent-based products are also harmless to plants when dry, but it makes sense to check before you buy.

Clear preservatives

You can use clear liquid preservers that protect timber from dry or wet rot only. Alternatively, use an all-purpose fluid that will also provide protection against wood-boring insects. Clear preservers are useful when you want to retain the appearance of natural timber – oak beams or hardwood doors, for example – and you can usually paint or varnish the surface once the wood has dried.

Green preserver

There is also a green solvent-based preserver that is traditionally used for horticultural timbers. Being coloured, it helps to identify treated timbers for the future. However, the colour is due to the presence of copper, which is not a permanent colouring agent when used outdoors. Nevertheless, its protective properties are unaffected, even when the colour is washed out by heavy rain.

Wood-coloured preservers

Tinted preservers are formulated to protect sound exterior timbers against fungal and insect attack while staining the wood at the same time.

There is a choice of brown shades intended to simulate the most common hardwoods, and one that is designed specifically to preserve the richness of cedarwood. Solvent-based preservers are made with light-fast pigments that inhibit fading. They do not penetrate as well as a clear preserver, but generally offer slightly better protection than the coloured water-based preservers.

Clear   Coloured   Green

SAFETY WITH PRESERVERS

Solvent-based preservers are flammable, so do not smoke while using them and extinguish any naked lights. Wear protective gloves and goggles when applying preservers, together with a respirator when using these liquids indoors. Provide good ventilation while working, and do not sleep in a freshly treated room for 48 hours or so – in order to allow time for the fumes to dissipate completely. Wash spilt preserver from your skin and eyes with water immediately, and do not delay seeking medical advice if irritation persists.

REFERENCE AND INDEX

Planning permission

Planning controls exist primarily to regulate the use and siting of buildings and other constructions as well as their appearance. What might seem to be a minor development in itself could have far-reaching implications you had not considered: a structure which obscured drivers' vision at a junction, for instance, might constitute a danger to traffic. Equally, the local authority might refuse permission on the grounds that the planned scheme does not blend sympathetically with its surroundings.

The actual details of planning requirements are complex but, in broad terms, with regard to domestic developments the planning authority is concerned with construction work such as an extension to the house or the provision of new outbuildings such as a garage. Structures like walls and fences fall into the same category because their height or siting might infringe the rights of other members of the community. The authority will also want to approve any change of use such as converting a house into flats or running a business from premises previously occupied as a dwelling only.

Your property may be affected by legal restrictions such as a right of way which might prejudice planning permission. Examine the deeds of your house or consult a solicitor.

Applying for planning permission

You can obtain the necessary application form from the planning department of your local council; it is laid out simply, with guidance notes to help you fill it in. Alternatively, ask a builder or architect to apply on your behalf. This is sensible if the development you are planning is in any way complicated, because you will have to include measured drawings with the application form. In all probability, you will have to prepare a plan showing the position of the site in question (site plan) so that the authority can determine exactly where the building is located. You must submit another, larger-scale, plan to show the relationship of the building to other premises and highways (block plan). In addition, you should supply drawings which give a clear idea of what the new proposal will look like, together with details of both the colour and the kind of materials you intend to use. You may prepare the drawings yourself, provided you are able to make them accurate.

Under normal circumstances you will have to pay a fee in order to seek planning permission, but there are exceptions. The planning department will advise you.

Before preparing detailed plans, you can make an outline application furnishing information on the size and form of the development. Assuming permission is granted under these circumstances, you will then have to submit a further application in greater detail. In the main, this applies to large-scale developments only and you will be better off making a full application in the first place.

Do not be afraid to discuss the proposal with a representative of the planning department before you submit your application. He or she will do his or her best to help you comply with the requirements and will always grant planning permission unless there are very sound reasons for refusal, in which case the department must explain the decision to you so that you can amend your plans accordingly and resubmit them for further consideration. A second application is normally exempt from a fee. As a last resort, however, you can appeal against a decision to the Secretary of State for the Environment. The planning authority will supply you with the necessary appeal forms. If you were to proceed without approval, you might find yourself obliged to restore the property to its original condition.

You can expect to receive a decision from the planning department within eight weeks and, once granted, planning permission is valid for five years. If the work is not begun within that time, you will have to apply for planning permission again.

Building Regulations

Even when planning permission is not required, most building works, including alterations to existing structures, are subject to minimum standards of construction to safeguard public health and safety. The Building Regulations are designed to ensure structural stability and to promote the use of suitable materials to provide adequate durability, fire and weather resistance, and the prevention of damp. The Regulations also stipulate the minimum amount of ventilation and natural light to be provided for habitable rooms.

Building standards are enforced by your local Building Control Officer, but for matters concerning drainage or sanitary installations, consult the Technical Services Department.

Obtaining approval

You, as the builder, are required to fill in an application form and return it, along with basic drawings and relevant information, to the Building Control Office at least two days before work commences. Alternatively, you may submit fully detailed plans for approval. Whatever method you adopt, it may save time and trouble if you make an appointment to discuss your scheme with the Building Control Officer well before you intend to carry out the work. He or she will be happy to discuss your intentions, including proposed structural details and dimensions, together with a list of the materials you intend to use so that he or she can point out any obvious contravention of the Regulations before you make an official application for approval. At the same time he or she can suggest whether it is necessary to approach other authorities to discuss planning, sanitation, fire escapes and so on. The Building Control Officer will ask you to inform the office when crucial stages of the work are ready for inspection by a surveyor in order to make sure the work is carried out according to your original specification. Should the surveyor be dissatisfied with any aspect of the work, he or she may suggest ways to remedy the situation.

If you wish, you can appoint a builder, or preferably an architect, to handle everything for you, but do not be bullied into ignoring the surveyor's request to inspect the site or you could incur the cost and inconvenience of exposing covered work at a later stage. Failure to submit an application form or detailed plans could result in a substantial fine as well as wasted time. You will be expected to pay certain fees to the local council for the services you have received from the surveyor. These fees are not extortionate and you can obtain an estimate of the amount before building begins.

When the building is finished you must notify the council, and it would be to your advantage to ask for written confirmation that the work was satisfactory as this will help to reassure a prospective buyer when you come to sell the property.

If you live in a single-family house you may undertake certain developments without planning permission. This chart is intended to help you decide whether you need to seek planning permission or Building Regulation approval before starting work. However, always check with the relevant authority for confirmation. If your dwelling has been converted to flats, all external alterations will require planning permission.

TYPE OF WORK	●	PLANNING PERMISSION		BUILDING REGULATION APPROVAL	
Decorations or repairs inside and outside	39 121	NO	Unless it is a listed building.	NO	
Replacing windows and doors	188 200	NO	Unless they project beyond the foremost wall of the house facing a highway. Or: The building is listed or is in a conservation area.	Possibly	Consult your Building Control Officer
Electrical work	292	NO		NO	But it must comply with IEE Regulations.
Plumbing	347	NO		NO / YES	No for replacements, but consult the Technical Services Department for any installation which alters present internal or external drainage. Yes for an unvented hot-water system.
Central heating	404	NO		NO	
Oil-storage tank		NO	Provided it is in the garden and has a capacity of not more than 3,500 litres (778 gallons). And: No point is more than 3m (9ft 9in) high. And: No part projects beyond the foremost wall of the house facing a highway.	NO	
Structural alterations inside	121	NO	As long as the use of the house is unchanged.	YES	
Loft conversion	157 273	NO / YES	No provided the volume of the house is unchanged, and the highest part of the roof is not raised. Yes for front-elevation dormer windows or rear ones over a certain size.	YES	
Building a garden wall or fence	424 434	YES	If it is more than 1m (3ft 3in) high and is a boundary enclosure adjoining a highway. Or: If it is more than 2m (6ft 6in) high elsewhere.	NO	
Planting a hedge		NO	Unless it obscures view of traffic at a junction or access to main road.	NO	
Laying a path or driveway	458	NO	Unless it provides access to main road.	NO	
Felling or lopping trees	423	NO	Unless the trees are protected or you live in a conservation area.	NO	
Installing a swimming pool	474	Possibly	Consult your planning department.	YES	For an indoor pool.
Constructing a small outbuilding	121 434	Possibly	*SEE MARGIN NOTE (RIGHT)*	YES	If area exceeds 30sq m (35.9sq yd). If it is within 1m (3ft 3in) of a boundary, it must be built from incombustible materials.
Building a porch	121 434	NO	Unless: The floor area exceeds 3sq m (3.6sq yd). Or: Any part is more than 3m (9ft 9in) high. Or: Any part is less than 2m (6ft 6in) from a boundary adjoining a highway or public footpath.	NO	If under 30sq m (35.9sq yd) in area.
Building a conservatory	475	Possibly	Treat as an extension	NO	If under 30sq m (35.9sq yd) in area.
Building a garage	121 434	YES	If within 5m (16ft 6in) of house, treat like an extension, otherwise treat as an outbuilding.	Possibly	Consult your Building Control Officer.
Hardstanding for a car	454	NO	Provided it is within your boundary and is not used for a commercial vehicle.	NO	
Building an extension	121 434	Possibly	You can extend your house up to certain permitted limits without planning permission (see margin note). However, the total of both previous and new extensions cannot exceed the permitted volume, or permission is required.	YES	
Demolition		YES	Particularly if it is listed or in a conservation area. And: If the whole house is to be demolished. Seek advice for partial demolition.	NO / YES	No for a complete, detached house. Yes for a partial demolition to ensure that the remaining part or adjoining buildings are structurally sound.
Converting a house to flats		YES	Including bedsitters	YES	
Converting a house to business premises		YES		YES	

● Refer to these pages for further information

● **OUTBUILDINGS**
You can build an outbuilding up to 10cu m (13.08cu yd) in volume without planning permission if it is within 5m (16ft 3in) of the house or an extension. Further away than this, it can be up to half the area of the garden, but the height must not exceed 4m (13ft).

● **EXTENSIONS**
Planning permission is required if:
Volume
The extension results in an increase in volume of the original house by whichever is the greater of the following amounts. For terraced houses 50cu m (65.5cu yd) or 10 per cent up to a maximum of 115cu m (150.4cu yd). Other houses 70cu m (91.5cu yd) or 15 per cent up to a maximum of 115cu m (150.4cu yd). In Scotland General category 24sq m (28.7sq yd) or 20 per cent.
Height
Any part is higher than the highest part of the house roof.
Projections
Any part projects beyond the foremost wall of the house facing a highway.
Boundary
Any part within 2m (6ft 6in) of a boundary is more than 4m (13ft) high.
Area
It will cover more than half the original area of the garden.
Dwelling
It is to be an independent dwelling.

73

BUILDING
TOOLS

Using a pointing hawk
A pointing hawk makes the filling of mortar joints very easy. Place the lip of the hawk just under a horizontal joint and scrape the mortar into place with a jointer.

Continental-pattern trowels

● **Essential tools**
Brick trowel
Pointing trowel
Plasterer's trowel
Mortar board
Hawk
Spirit level
Try square
Plumb line

BUILDER'S TOOL KIT

A specialist builder – such as a plasterer, joiner or bricklayer – needs only a limited set of tools, whereas the amateur is more like a one-man general builder, who has to be able to tackle all kinds of construction and repair work, and therefore requires a much wider range of tools than the specialist.

The tool kit suggested here is for renovating and improving the structure of your home and for such tasks as erecting or restoring garden structures and laying paving. Electrical work, decorating and plumbing call for other sets of tools.

FLOATS AND TROWELS

For a professional builder, floats and trowels have their specific uses – but in home maintenance a repointing trowel may often be the ideal tool for patching small areas of plaster, or a plasterer's trowel for smoothing concrete.

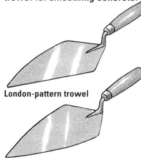

London-pattern trowel

Canadian-pattern trowel

Brick trowels
A brick trowel is for handling and placing mortar when laying bricks or concrete blocks. A professional might use one with a blade as long as 300mm (1ft) – but such a trowel is too heavy and unwieldy for the amateur, so buy a good-quality brick trowel with a fairly short blade.

The blade of a **London-pattern trowel** has one curved edge for cutting bricks, a skill that takes much practice to perfect; the blade's other edge is straight, for picking up mortar. This type of trowel is made in right-handed and left-handed versions, so be sure to buy the right one for you. A right-handed trowel has its curved edge on the right when you are holding the tool.

A **Canadian-pattern trowel** is symmetrical, so it's convenient when people with different left-hand and right-hand preferences want to share the one trowel.

Pointing trowel
A pointing trowel is designed for repairing or shaping mortar joints between bricks. The blade is only 75 to 100mm (3 to 4in) long.

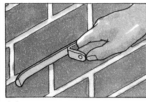

Jointer
Use a jointer to shape the mortar joints between bricks. Its narrow blade is dragged along the mortar joint and the curved front end used for shaping the verticals.

Frenchman
A Frenchman is a specialized tool for scraping off excess mortar from brickwork jointing. You can make one by heating and bending an old table knife or a metal strip.

Wooden float
A wooden builder's float is for applying and smoothing cement renderings and concrete to a fine, attractive texture. The more expensive ones have detachable handles, so their wooden blades can be replaced when they wear. Similar floats made from plastic are also available.

Plasterer's trowel
A plasterer's trowel is a steel float for applying plaster and cement renderings to walls. It is also dampened and used for 'polishing', stroking the surface of the material when it has firmed up. Some builders prefer to apply rendering with a heavy trowel and finish it with a more flexible blade – but one has to be quite skilled to exploit such subtle differences.

BOARDS FOR CARRYING MORTAR OR PLASTER

Any convenient-sized sheet of 12 or 18mm (½ or ¾in) exterior-grade plywood can be used as a mixing board for plaster or mortar. A panel about 1m (3ft) square makes an ideal mixing board, while a smaller spot-board, about 600mm (2ft) square, is convenient for carrying the material to the actual work site. Screwing some battens to the underside of the boards makes them easier to lift and carry.

You will also need a small lightweight hawk for carrying pointing mortar or plaster. Make one by nailing a block of wood underneath a plywood board so you can plug a handle into it.

A home-made hawk

LEVELLING AND MEASURING TOOLS

You can make some levelling and measuring tools yourself – but don't skimp on essentials, such as a good spirit level and a robust tape measure.

VIAL

Spirit level
A spirit level is a machine-made straightedge incorporating special glass tubes or vials that contain a liquid. In each vial an air bubble floats. When a bubble rests exactly between two lines marked on the glass, then the structure on which the level is held is known to be properly horizontal or vertical, depending on the orientation of the vial.

Buy a wooden or lightweight aluminium level, 600 to 900mm (2 to 3ft) long. A well-made one is very strong, but treat it with care and always clean mortar or plaster from it before they set.

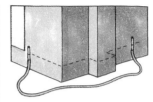

Water level
You can make a water level by plugging short lengths of transparent plastic tubing into the two ends of a garden hose; fill the hose with water till it appears in both tubes. Since water level remains constant, the levels in the tubes are always identical and can therefore be used for marking identical heights, even over long distances and round obstacles and bends.

Builder's square
A large set square is useful when you set out brick or concrete-block corners. The best squares are stamped out of sheet metal, but you can make a serviceable one by cutting out a thick plywood right-angled triangle with a hypotenuse of about 750mm (2ft 6in). Cut out the centre of the triangle to reduce the weight.

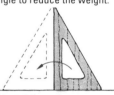

Checking a square
Accuracy is important, so check the square by placing it against a straight batten on the floor. Draw a line against the square to make a right angle with the batten, then flop the square to see if it forms the same angle from the other side.

Try square
Use a try square for marking out square cuts or joints on timber.

Making a plumb line
Any small heavy weight hung on a length of fine string can act as a plumb line for judging whether a structure or surface is vertical.

BUILDING TOOLS

Bricklayer's line

This is a nylon line used as a guide for laying bricks or blocks level. It is stretched between two flat-bladed pins that are driven into vertical joints at the ends of a wall, or between line blocks that hook over the bricks at the ends of a course. As a substitute, you can stretch string between two stakes driven into the ground outside the line of the wall.

Steel pins and line
Buy the special flat-bladed pins, or make your own by hammering flats on 100mm (4in) nails.

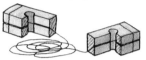

Line blocks
The blocks grip the corners of the bricks at the end of a course; the line passes through their slots.

Plasterer's rule

This is simply a straight length of wood used for scraping plaster and rendering undercoats level.

Straightedge

Any length of straight rigid timber can be used to check whether a surface is flat, or (in conjunction with a spirit level) to see whether two points are at the same height.

Gauge stick

For gauging the height of brick courses, calibrate a softwood batten by making sawcuts across it at 75mm (3in) intervals – which is the thickness of a brick plus its mortar joint.

Tape measure

An ordinary retractable steel tape measure is adequate for most purposes; but if you need to mark out or measure a large plot, hire a wind-up tape – which can be up to 30m (100ft) in length.

Marking gauge

A marking gauge has a sharp steel point for scoring a line on timber parallel to the edge. Its adjustable stock acts as a fence and keeps the point a constant distance from the edge.

HAMMERS

Several types of hammer are useful on a building site.

Claw hammer

Choose a strong claw hammer for building stud partitions, nailing floorboards, making doorframes and window frames, and putting up garden fencing.

Club hammer

A heavy club hammer is used for driving cold chisels and for a variety of demolition jobs. It is also useful for driving large masonry nails into walls.

Sledgehammer

Hire a sledgehammer if you have to break up hardcore or paving. It's also the best tool for driving stakes or fence posts into the ground, though you can make do with a club hammer if the ground is not too hard.

Mallet

A carpenter's wooden mallet is the proper tool for driving a wood chisel. But you can use a hammer instead if the chisel has an impact-resistant plastic handle.

SAWS

Every builder needs a range of handsaws, but consider hiring a power saw when you have to cut a lot of heavy structural timbers – especially if you plan to rip floorboards down to width, which is a very tiring job when done by hand.

Special saws are available for cutting metal, and even for sawing through masonry.

Panel saw

All kinds of man-made building boards are used in house construction, so it is worth investing in a good panel saw.

It can also be used for cutting large structural timbers to the required lengths.

Tenon saw

This is a good saw for accurately cutting wall studs, floorboards, panelling and joints. The metal stiffening along the top of the blade keeps it rigid and prevents the saw from wandering off line.

Padsaw

Also called a keyhole saw, this small saw has a narrow tapered blade for cutting holes in timber.

Coping saw

A coping saw has a frame that holds a fairly coarse but very narrow blade under tension for cutting curves in wood.

Floorboard saw

If you prise a floorboard above its neighbours, you can cut across it with an ordinary tenon saw – but the curved cutting edge of a floorboard saw makes it easier to avoid damaging the boards on either side.

Hacksaw

The hardened-steel blades of a hacksaw have fine teeth for cutting metal. Use one to cut steel concrete-reinforcing rods or small pieces of sheet metal.

Sheet saw

A hacksaw's frame prevents its use for cutting large metal sheets – but a sheet saw has a replaceable hacksaw blade bolted to the edge of a flat blade that can pass through the sheet like a handsaw. It will also cut corrugated plastic sheeting and roofing slates.

Universal saw

A universal or general-purpose saw is able to cut wood, metal, plastics and building boards. The short frameless blade has a low-friction coating.

This type of saw is particularly useful for cutting secondhand timber, which may contain nails or screws that would blunt the blade of an ordinary woodsaw.

POWER SAWS

A *circular saw* will accurately rip timber or man-made boards down to size. As well as saving you the effort of hand-sawing large timbers, a sharp power saw produces such a clean cut that there is often no need for planing afterwards.

A *power jigsaw* is able to cut curves in timber and boards. It is equally useful for cutting holes in fixed wall panels and for sawing through floorboards.

A *reciprocating saw* is a two-handed power saw that has a long pointed blade. It is powerful enough to saw sections of heavy timber, and can even cut through a complete stud partition.

Masonry saw

Masonry saws closely resemble handsaws for wood, but their tungsten-carbide teeth cut brick, concrete blocks and stone.

DRILLS

A powerful electric drill is invaluable to a builder. A cordless version is useful when you have to bore holes outdoors or in lofts and cellars that lack convenient electric sockets.

Power drill

Buy a good-quality power drill, plus a range of twist drills and spade or power-bore bits for drilling timber. Make sure the drill has a percussion or hammer action for drilling walls. For masonry you need special drill bits tipped with tungsten carbide. The smaller ones are matched to the size of standard wall plugs; there are also much larger ones that have reduced shanks, so they can be used in a standard power-drill chuck. The larger bits are expensive, so it pays to hire them. Percussion bits are even tougher than masonry bits, and have shatter-proof tips.

Brace

A brace is the ideal hand tool for drilling large holes in timber. In addition, when fitted with a screwdriver bit, it provides the necessary leverage for inserting or extracting large woodscrews.

Drilling masonry for wall plugs
Set the drill to hammer action and low speed. Wrap tape round the bit to mark the depth to be drilled, allowing for slightly more depth than the length of the plug, as dust will pack down into the hole as the plug is inserted. Drill the hole in stages, partly withdrawing the bit at times in order to clear the debris.

To protect paintwork and floorcoverings from falling dust, tape a paper bag just below the position of the hole before starting drilling.

● **Essential tools**
Straightedge
Tape measure
Claw hammer
Club hammer
Panel saw
Tenon saw
Hacksaw
Padsaw
Power drill
Masonry bits
Brace and bits

BUILDING
TOOLS

**ADDITIONAL
BUILDER'S TOOLS
The following tools
would be a useful
addition to a builder's
tool kit, especially
when carrying out
major repairs and
improvements:**

Crowbar
A crowbar, or
wrecking bar, is for
demolishing timber
framework. Force the
flat tip between the
components and use
the leverage of the
long shaft to prise
them apart. Choose a
crowbar that has a
claw at one end for
removing large nails.

Slater's ripper
To replace individual
slates you must cut
their fixing nails
without disturbing the
slates overlapping
them, and for this you
need a slater's ripper.
Pass the long hooked
blade up between the
slates, locate one
of the hooks over the
fixing nail, and pull
down sharply to cut it.

● **Essential tools**
Glass cutter
Putty knife
Cold chisel
Bolster chisel
Spade
Shovel
Rake
Wheelbarrow
Cabinet screwdriver
Cross-head
screwdriver
Jack plane

GLAZIER'S TOOLS

*Glass is such a hard and brittle
material that it can only be
worked with specialized tools.*

Glass cutter
A glass cutter does not actually
cut glass, but merely scores a
line in it. This is done by a tiny
hardened-steel wheel or a chip
of industrial diamond mounted
in the pen-like holder. The glass
breaks along the scored line
when pressure is applied to it.

Beam compass cutter
A beam compass cutter is for
scoring circles on glass – when,
for example, you need to cut
a round hole in a window pane
in order to fit a ventilator. The
cutting wheel is mounted at the
end of an adjustable beam that
turns on a central pivot attached
to the glass by suction.

Spear-point glass drill
A glass drill has a flat tungsten-
steel tip shaped like a spearhead.
The shape of the tip is designed
to reduce friction that would
otherwise crack the glass, but it
does need lubricating with oil,
paraffin or water during drilling.

Hacking knife
A hacking knife has a heavy steel
blade for chipping old putty out
of window rebates in order to
remove the glass. Place the point
between the putty and the frame,
then tap the back of the blade
with a hammer.

Spearpoint knife

Clipped-point knife

Straight knife

Putty knife
The blunt blade of a putty knife is
for shaping and smoothing fresh
putty. You can choose between
spearpoint, clipped-point and
straight blades according to your
personal preference.

CHISELS

*As well as chisels for cutting
and paring wood joints, you will
need some special ones when
working with masonry.*

Cold chisel
Cold chisels are made from solid-
steel hexagonal-section rod. They
are primarily for cutting metal
bars and chopping the heads off
rivets, but a builder will use one
for cutting a chase in plaster and
brickwork or for chopping out old
brick pointing.

Slip a plastic safety sleeve
over the chisel to protect your
hand from a misplaced blow with
a club hammer.

Plugging chisel
A plugging chisel has a narrow,
flat 'bit' (tip) for cutting out old or
eroded pointing. It's worth hiring
one when you have a large area
of brickwork to repoint.

Bolster chisel
The wide 'bit' of a bolster chisel
is designed for cutting bricks and
concrete blocks. It is also useful
for levering up floorboards.

WORK GLOVES

**Wear strong work gloves when-
ever you are carrying paving
slabs, concrete blocks or rough
timber. Ordinary gardening
gloves are better than none, but
they won't last very long on a
building site. The best work
gloves have leather palms and
fingers, although you may prefer
a pair with ventilated backs for
comfort in hot weather.**

DIGGING TOOLS

*Much building work requires
some kind of digging – for laying
strip foundations and concrete
pads, sinking rows of post holes,
and so on. You probably have
the basic tools in your garden
shed; the others you can hire.*

Pickaxe
Use a medium-weight pickaxe to
break up heavily compacted soil
– especially if it contains a lot of
buried rubble.

Mattock
The wide blade of a mattock
is ideal for breaking up heavy
clay soil, and it's better than
an ordinary pickaxe for ground
that's riddled with tree roots.

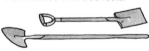

Spade
Buy a good-quality spade for
excavating soil and mixing
concrete. One with a stainless-
steel blade is best, but alloy steel
lasts reasonably well. Choose
a strong hardwood shaft split to
form a D-shaped handle that is
riveted with metal plates to its
crosspiece. Make sure that the
hollow shaft socket and blade
are forged in one piece.

Although square spade blades
seem to be more popular, many
builders prefer a round-mouth
spade with a long pole handle for
digging deep holes and trenches.

Shovel
You can use a spade for mixing
and placing concrete or mortar,
but the raised edges of a shovel
retain it better.

Garden rake
Use an ordinary garden rake for
spreading gravel or levelling wet
concrete, but be sure to wash it
before any concrete sets on it.

Post-hole auger
Hire a post-hole auger to sink
narrow holes for fence and gate
posts. You drive it into the ground
like a corkscrew, then pull out
the plugs of earth.

Wheelbarrow
Most garden wheelbarrows are
not strong enough for building
work, which generally involves
carting heavy loads of rubble and
wet concrete.

Unless the tubular underframe
of the wheelbarrow is rigidly
strutted, the barrow's thin metal
body will distort and may well
spill its load as you are crossing
rough ground.

Check, too, that the axle is
fixed securely – a cheap barrow
can lose its wheel as you are
tipping a load into an excavation.

SCREWDRIVERS

*Most people gradually acquire
an assortment of screwdrivers
over a period of time, as and
when need arises. Alternatively,
buy a power screwdriver with a
range of bits or buy screwdriver
bits for your power drill.*

Cabinet screwdriver
Buy at least one large flat-tip
screwdriver. The fixed variety is
quite adequate, but a pump-
action one, which drives large
screws very quickly, is useful
when you assemble big wooden
building structures.

Cross-head screwdriver
Choose the size and type of
cross-head screwdriver to suit
the work in hand. There is no
'most-useful size', as each driver
must fit a screw slot exactly.

PLANES

*Sophisticated framing may call
for moulding or grooving planes,
but most household joinery
needs only skimming to leave a
fairly smooth finish.*

Jack plane
A jack plane, which is a medium-
size bench plane, is the most
versatile general-purpose tool.

GLOSSARY
OF TERMS

Aggregate
Particles of sand or stone mixed with cement and water to make concrete.

Alkali-resistant primer
A primer used to prevent the alkali content of building materials attacking a coating of solvent-based paint.

Aluminium sealer
A paint designed to obliterate materials likely to 'bleed' through subsequent coatings.

Ballast
A naturally occurring mixture of sand and gravel used for making concrete.

Batter
The slope of the face of a wall that leans backwards or tapers from bottom to top.

Blown
To have broken away, as when a layer of rendering has parted from a wall.

Bond
A staggered pattern of bricks designed to spread the static load along a wall and to tie the individual units together.

Boundary wall
A wall that defines the line or limit of an area of property.

Capping strip
A length of timber nailed to the top edge of a fence panel.

Cavity insulation
A thermal-insulating material introduced to the void within a cavity wall to slow down the transmission of heat.

Cavity tray
A sloping membrane built within a cavity wall to shed moisture to the outer skin, preventing damp permeating to the inside of the house.

Cavity wall
A wall built with two skins of masonry separated by a gap to prevent the passage of moisture through the wall to the interior.

Cleat
A short length of timber used to join two longer pieces end to end by being nailed across the butt joint.

Control joint
A continuous joint built into a wall or concrete base to allow for expansion.

Coping
The top course of bricks or slabs of a wall, designed to shed rainwater to prevent moisture seeping into the upper joints of the masonry.

Counterbore
To cut a hole which allows the head of a bolt or screw to lie below a surface. *or* The hole itself.

Damp-proof course – DPC
A layer of impervious material which prevents moisture rising from the ground into the walls of a building.

Damp-proof membrane – DPM
A layer of impervious material which prevents moisture rising through a concrete floor.

Datum point
The point from which measurements are taken.

Doorframe
The lining of timber used to finish the inner edges of a masonry door opening.

Door lintel
The beam of reinforced concrete or timber that supports the masonry above a door opening.

Dressing
The process of finishing the faces of stone blocks.

Drip groove
A groove cut or moulded in the underside of a door or window sill to prevent water running back to the wall.

Efflorescence
A white powdery deposit caused by soluble salts migrating to the surface of a wall or ceiling.

Featherboarding
Strips of wood with a tapered section, used as components for a closeboard fence.

Footing
A narrow concrete foundation for a wall.

Frass
Powdered wood produced by the activity of woodworm.

Hardcore
Broken bricks or stones used to form a sub-base below foundations, paving etc.

Heave
An upward swelling of the ground caused by excess moisture.

Hoggin
A fine ballast, usually with a clay content, used to form a sub-base for concrete pads or paving.

IEE Regulations
A code of professional practice laid down by the Institution of Electrical Engineers.

Lead
A stepped section of brick- or blockwork built at each end of a wall to serve as a guide to the height of intermediate coursing.

Marine plywood
Exterior-grade plywood.

Mastic
A nonsetting compound used to seal joints.

Masonry bolt
A fixing device designed to anchor itself in a masonry wall by expansion.

Moisture-vapour permeable
A property of a finish which allows timber to dry out while protecting it from rainwater.

Pale
An upright member of a fence, often cut with a pointed or rounded end.

Pavers
Small bricks or concrete blocks used to form a durable surface for a drive or path.

Penetrating damp
Moisture which permeates the fabric of a house due to faulty building techniques or disrepair.

Piers
Columns of masonry used to form a gateway or buttress a wall at regular intervals.

Primer
The first coat of a traditional paint system. A primer protects the workpiece and reduces absorption of subsequent coats.

Render
A thin layer of cement-based mortar applied to exterior walls to provide a protective finish. Sometimes fine stone aggregate is embedded in the mortar. *or* To apply this type of mortar.

Retaining wall
A wall built against a bank of earth to prevent it slipping.

Riven
Split or cleaved.

Scratchcoat
The bottom layer of cement render.

Set
A small rectangular paving block.

Shim
A thin packing strip.

Skew nailing
A secure fixing achieved by driving nails dovetail-fashion.

Soakaway
A pit filled with rubble or gravel into which water is drained.

Spalling
Flaking of the outer face of masonry caused by expanding moisture in icy conditions.

Spur
A short wooden or concrete stake to support a fence post. *or* A length of electrical cable that feeds a socket outlet or fused connection unit by taking its power via another similar accessory.

Stud partition
An interior timber-framed dividing wall.

Subsidence
A sinking of the ground caused by the shrinkage of excessively dry soil.

Tamp
To pack down firmly with repeated blows.

Transformer
A device which increases or decreases voltage on an electrical circuit.

Weep hole
A small hole at the base of a cavity wall to allow absorbed water to drain to the outside.